COOKIES

COOKIES

OVER 70 CLASSIC AND CREATIVE COOKIE RECIPES

CONTENTS

Introduction

Every home should have a well-stocked jar of cookies ready and waiting to be dipped into. Cookies are easy and enjoyable to make and they are great for sharing over a midmorning cup of coffee or afternoon tea break. They're made in individual servings (although it can be difficult to stop after eating just one), and there's no hassle with cutting or spooning up to serve.

The beauty of homemade cookies is that you can customize them for any occasion or celebration. Using cookie cutters to create shapes or adding simple icings and decorations, you can create artistic masterpieces that look just as good as they taste.

No matter what flavor of cookie you choose or how you decide to adorn them, making delicious cookies is a breeze and decorating them is much easier than you might imagine. Just follow the simple recipes, helpful tips, and step-by-step decorating directions in this book and you'll soon be whipping up batches of perfectly baked cookies.

Once you've mastered the basic recipes and techniques, the sky's the limit. All you need is a dash of imagination and you'll be able to create cookies to suit any occasion. Happy baking, decorating, and, of course, devouring!

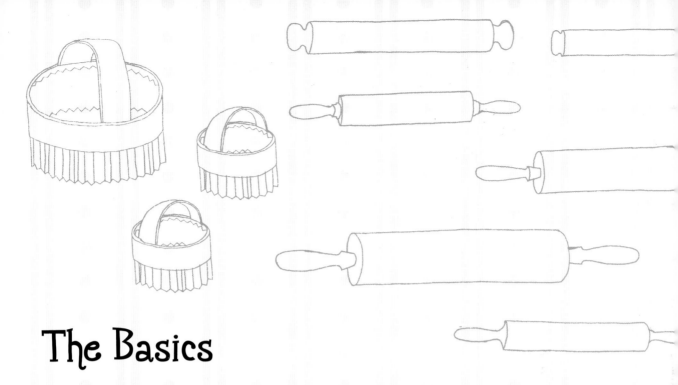

The Basics

Whether they're soft and chewy, crisp and crumbly, covered in fancy icing, or filled with special ingredients, most of the cookies in this book are either cutout, sliced, drop, or piped cookies.

Cutout cookies

These cookies are defined by their cut shapes, created by using a cookie cutter. The dough is often chilled before being rolled out, and again before it is baked. This helps the cookies to keep their shape and minimizes spreading in the oven.

Sliced cookies

As the name suggests, sliced cookies are created when dough is rolled into a long log shape and sliced to create the individual cookies.

Drop cookies

Drop cookies have a more textured, wetter dough than other cookie dough types, and they often include added ingredients, such as nuts or chocolate chips. The dough is spooned onto baking sheets before baking.

Piped cookies

Piped cookies are made by spooning the soft cookie dough into a pastry bag fitted with a large tip and by piping it in various shapes onto the baking sheets. Alternatively, a cookie press—which looks a little like a caulking gun—may be used. It can be fitted with disks of varying designs to create cookies that are decoratively shaped.

The Star Ingredients

Fat, sugar, eggs, and flour are the basic ingredients for most cookie recipes, so they are useful ingredients to have on hand if you're serious about getting into making cookies.

Fat

Butter is the ideal fat for making cookies, giving them a rich flavor that margarine cannot match. Unsalted butter is always best for sweet baking. However, if you prefer to use margarine, make sure to use one that is described on the package as suitable for baking.

Sugar

Professionals prefer superfine because it dissolves more easily than granulated sugar. If you have only granulated sugar, you can process it in a food processor for 60 seconds to make superfine sugar. Brown sugar is used in some recipes to provide a richer flavor. Confectioners' sugar, or powdered sugar, is used to make icings and buttercream. It can also be dusted over cookies to decorate them.

Eggs

Unless otherwise stated, the size of the eggs used in the recipes is large. If possible, use eggs at room temperature, because cold eggs may cause curdling and will result in a less soft mixture.

Flour

The flour used in the recipes is all-purpose flour. It is not necessary to sift flour unless you are combining several dry ingredients.

Additional ingredients, such as flavoring extracts, dried fruits, nuts, and chocolate, will add flavor and texture and are what turn a basic cookie into something extraordinary!

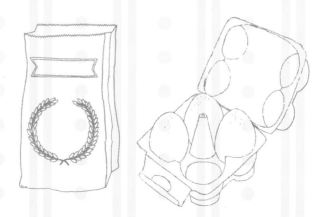

Essential Equipment

You won't need loads of expensive equipment or speciality cooking tools to make cookies, but there are a few essentials.

Baking sheets

It is worth investing in a few good-quality baking sheets because cheaper ones have a tendency to buckle in the oven and may not distribute heat evenly. It may sound obvious, but do check the dimensions of your oven before buying baking sheets.

Parchment paper

Parchment paper has a shiny, nonstick surface. Its main use is to line baking sheets to prevent cookies from sticking to them, but it's also useful when rolling out cookie dough—by placing the dough between two sheets of baking paper, you eliminate the need to add additional flour and thus avoid upsetting the balance of ingredients. Parchment paper can also be used to make paper pastry bags (see page 11) and to place decorated cookies on while they dry.

Electric mixer

An electric mixer is useful for beating ingredients together, but you could use a wire whisk for whisking and a wooden spoon for creaming.

Rolling pin

This is a useful piece of equipment if you want to make rolled cookies, but there are plenty of cookies you can still make if you don't have one.

Cookie cutters

Again, these are for using with rolled cookies and are not strictly essential, but there is such a range of shapes and sizes available that you might be tempted to buy some anyway. If you don't have a cookie cutter in the desired shape, it's easy to make a template out of cardboard. Simply place the template on top of the rolled cookie dough and cut around it with a small, sharp knife.

Wire racks

Wire racks are handy for cooling your cookies. The design allows for air to circulate around the cookies, preventing them from becoming soggy.

Pastry bags and tips

There are plenty of ways to ice and decorate cookies without needing a pastry bag or tip, but you might want to consider investing in a small set if you want to try the more elaborate designs in this book.

Icing Masterclass

Icing is the final flourish when it comes to your home-baked cookies, and it can add color and flavor to your baking. Knowing which type of icing is best for your latest batch of baking is essential if you want to add the wow factor.

Royal icing
Made with confectioners' sugar, egg whites (or egg white powder) and water (or lemon juice), this is the go-to icing for creating works of art on your cookies. It can be used to pipe the outline of the desired shape on a cookie, and then watered down slightly to fill or "flood" the area inside the outline to make a solid shape. Once set, royal icing creates a hard, smooth surface that's perfect for decorating with edible markers or food coloring "paint." You can, of course, create colored royal icing and, because of its long setting time, it's possible to create all kinds of impressive effects (like polka dots or feathering) just by combining a mixture of colors.

Glaze
The simplest icing of all—a glaze is basically a mixture of confectioners' sugar and water or other liquid, such as food coloring. It can be mixed to a thin consistency for a light glaze on a cookie, or beaten until thick and smooth for more controlled decorations. A simple glaze is great for attaching other decorations to your cookies, or for adding a burst of sweetness to your baking.

Fondant
The appeal of ready-to-use fondant is that it can be colored, rolled, cut, molded, and shaped into all kinds of designs to give a polished look to your cookies. Some people aren't enthusiastic about the taste of fondant, but it can be flavored, using concentrated flavoring oils or extracts.

There's no need to go to the trouble of making your own fondant because ready-to-use fondant is available from specialty cake suppliers and online. To color fondant yourself, use gel or paste food coloring to achieve vibrant hues without affecting the consistency by adding liquid.

Buttercream
This fluffy frosting is made from butter and confectioners' sugar, beaten until it's soft and light. Buttercream can be spread with a spatula or piped and is ideal as a filling for sandwich cookies.

Piping Perfection

Pastry bags, usually used in conjunction with piping tips, are extremely handy for piping icing, frosting, or even, in the case of piped cookies, for piping the cookie dough itself. Whether you choose to use reusable or disposable pastry bags, make sure to suit the size of the bag to the job. For piping cookie dough or buttercream, use large bags that have plenty of room for filling. For royal icing or a glaze, use a small or medium bag.

Paper pastry bags are handy if you have a number of icings in different colors on the go at one time. To make a small paper pastry bag, fold a 10-inch square of parchment paper diagonally in half, then hold the two points at each end of the long edge. Curl one point over to meet the center point, making a cone shape, then curl the other point over so that all three points meet. Fold the points over a couple of times to secure the cone. Snip off the end and use with or without a piping tip. You can also use a heavy-duty plastic food bag as a pastry bag by snipping off the corner and inserting a piping tip, if desired.

To fill a pastry bag, cut off about ½ inch from the tip and insert your piping tip inside the bag. Fold the sides down over your hand (or you can place the bag in a tall glass, folding the bag down over the sides) and, using the other hand, scoop in the icing, frosting, or cookie dough using a spatula. Do not overfill the bag; you need to leave enough space at the top to twist it tightly closed. To use, gently squeeze the bag from the top and move the tip to create the desired shape or outline.

Piping tips come in dozens of shapes and sizes. You can buy them separately or in sets. A fine plain tip will come in handy if you want to decorate your cookies with royal icing, while larger plain or shaped tips are useful for making piped cookies or creating decorative effects with buttercream.

The Secrets To Success

There's something extra-special about a home-baked cookie—nothing beats eating still-warm treats, fresh from the oven and made by your own hand. To many, baking at home can seem a daunting prospect, but it's easy. As long as you put in the necessary preparation work beforehand and exercise patience while working through the recipe, you will be richly rewarded by the results.

Before

• Prepare your kitchen by clearing work surfaces and getting out any equipment you may need.

• Check that you have all the ingredients for the recipe you want to make—there is nothing worse than finding out that you've run out of something halfway through baking.

• Unless otherwise instructed, remove your eggs and butter from the refrigerator about an hour before you begin. This allows for the eggs to come up to room temperature and the butter to soften.

• Read the recipe all the way through so there are no surprises.

• Line or grease any baking sheets as per the recipe.

• Preheat the oven for 10–15 minutes. If you have a convection oven, reduce the temperature according to the manufacturer's instructions.

• Measure out the ingredients carefully, making sure the ingredients are level in either the cup or spoon.

During

• Clean up as you work: wipe down work surfaces, put away ingredients, and neatly stack dirty dishes for later.

• Follow the chilling, cooling, or setting times specified—they're there for a reason, and are the perfect excuse for a mid-baking coffee break.

• Always place the cookie dough on cold baking sheets to prevent the dough from spreading excessively and browning too much around the edges.

• Space cookies well apart on the baking sheet to allow room for them to spread during cooking, otherwise your cookies may merge together and you could end up with one large cookie.

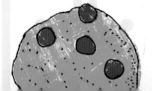

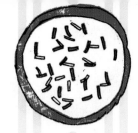

• Don't peek in the oven until the minimum baking time is reached. Opening the door of the oven lets the heat out and may affect the final consistency of your cookies.

After

• Unless otherwise instructed, transfer cookies to a wire rack as soon as they are firm enough to handle. This will allow for steam to evaporate and stop your cookies from turning soggy.

• Let cookies cool completely before storing in airtight containers or decorating them.

Storage

Cookies are, of course, at their best when freshly baked. With a few exceptions, most of the cookies in this book will keep well in a cookie jar or other airtight container. The following tips, however, will help:

• Always cool cookies completely before storing in airtight containers, otherwise they are liable to stick together.

• Ideally, store baked cookies undecorated; most undecorated cookies will keep in an airtight container for up to a week. Cookies decorated with a glaze, royal icing, or fondant can be stored for up to three days. Cookies frosted with buttercream should be eaten the day they are made.

• Store soft types of cookies separately from crisp ones so that they don't all become soft.

• One or two sugar cubes added to a container of cookies will help to keep them crisp.

• Unfrosted cookies can also be frozen, in a single layer in a sealed container, for up to three months. Ice them while they are still frozen, and then defrost in the refrigerator for several hours. Bring to room temperature before serving.

• The cookie dough for many sliced cookies (for example, the Refrigerator Cookies on page 30) may be stored in the refrigerator or freezer and slices cut off and baked as and when required—very convenient if you want a couple of freshly baked cookies in a hurry.

• Most frostings, too, can be refrigerated or frozen. Buttercream can be stored in a tightly covered container in the refrigerator for up to two weeks or in the freezer for six months. Thaw frozen frosting in the refrigerator and beat it with an electric mixer for a minute or two before using.

• Ready-to-use fondant can be stored indefinitely in a cool, dark place if wrapped tightly.

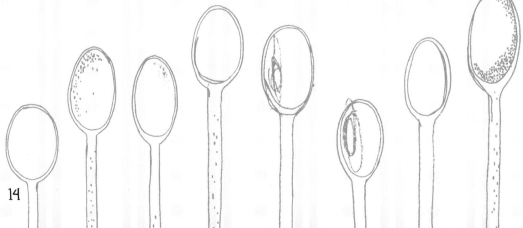

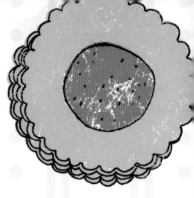

CHAPTER 1

COOKIE JAR FAVORITES

Chocolate Chip Cookies

makes 8

ingredients

1 ⅓ cups all-purpose flour

1 teaspoon baking powder

1 stick butter or ½ cup margarine, melted, plus extra for greasing

⅓ cup firmly packed light brown sugar

¼ cup superfine sugar or granulated sugar

½ teaspoon vanilla extract

1 egg, beaten

¾ cup semisweet chocolate chips

1. Preheat the oven to 375°F. Lightly grease two baking sheets.

2. Sift the flour and baking powder into a large mixing bowl. Add the remaining ingredients and beat until well combined.

3. Place tablespoons of the dough on the prepared baking sheets, spaced well apart.

4. Bake in the preheated oven for 10–12 minutes, or until golden brown. Let cool on the baking sheets for a few minutes, then transfer to a wire rack to cool completely.

1

2

3

Classic Oatmeal Cookies

makes 30

ingredients

1½ sticks unsalted butter,
softened, plus extra
for greasing

1⅓ cups demerara sugar or
other raw brown sugar

1 egg, beaten

¼ cup water

1 teaspoon vanilla extract

1¼ cups all-purpose flour

1 teaspoon salt

½ teaspoon baking soda

4 cups rolled oats

1. Preheat the oven to 350°F. Lightly grease two large baking sheets.

2. Put the butter and sugar into a large bowl and beat together until pale and creamy. Beat in the egg, water, and vanilla extract until the mixture is smooth.

3. Sift the flour, salt, and baking soda into a separate mixing bowl and mix in the oats, then gradually stir the oat mixture into the creamed mixture until thoroughly combined.

4. Place tablespoonfuls of the mixture on the prepared baking sheets, spaced well apart.

5. Bake in the preheated oven for 15 minutes, or until golden brown. Let cool on the baking sheets for a few minutes, then transfer to wire racks to cool completely.

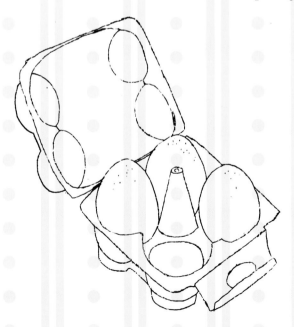

2

3

4

Vanilla Sugar Cookies

makes 24

ingredients

1¾ sticks unsalted butter, softened

¾ cup superfine sugar or granulated sugar

1 extra-large egg

2 teaspoons vanilla extract

3¼ cups all-purpose flour

clear cellophane plastic sheet and colorful ribbons, for wrapping (optional)

1. Line two baking sheets with parchment paper.

2. In a large bowl, cream the butter and sugar with an electric mixer until just coming together. Add the egg and vanilla extract and briefly beat together.

3. Add the flour and use a wooden spoon to mix everything together to make a coarse dough. Gather into a ball with your hands, wrap in plastic wrap, and chill in the refrigerator for at least 10 minutes.

4. Unwrap the dough and roll out between two large sheets of parchment paper, turning the dough occasionally until it is an even thickness of about ¼ inch. Stamp out about 24 shapes using a 3¼-inch star-shape cutter, rerolling the dough as necessary.

5. Transfer the cookies to the prepared baking sheets. Chill in the refrigerator for 10 minutes. Meanwhile, preheat the oven to 350°F.

6. Bake in the preheated oven for 15–18 minutes, or until just turning golden at the edges. Let cool on the baking sheets for a few minutes, then transfer to wire racks to cool completely.

7. If you would like to give the cookies as a gift, stack them into piles, wrap in cellophane, and tie with ribbon.

3

4

6

Danish Butter Cookies

makes 14

ingredients

1 stick unsalted butter, softened

⅓ cup confectioners' sugar, plus extra for dusting (optional)

1 cup all-purpose flour

¼ teaspoon baking powder

1. Preheat the oven to 375°F. Line two baking sheets with parchment paper.

2. Place the butter in a large bowl and beat with a wooden spoon until soft and pale. Sift in the confectioners' sugar and beat until smooth. Sift in the flour and baking powder and beat together to form a soft and sticky dough.

3. Spoon the dough into a pastry bag fitted with a ½-inch fluted tip. Pipe 14 wreath shapes onto the prepared baking sheet.

4. Bake in the preheated oven for 10–12 minutes, or until set and pale golden around the edges. Let cool on the baking sheets for a few minutes, then transfer to wire racks to cool completely. Dust with confectioners' sugar, if desired.

2

3

3

Peanut Butter Cookies

makes 15

ingredients

1⅓ cups all-purpose flour

½ teaspoon baking powder

½ teaspoon salt

1 cup smooth peanut butter

1 stick unsalted butter, softened, plus extra for greasing

1¼ teaspoons vanilla extract

⅔ cup firmly packed light brown sugar

½ cup superfine sugar or granulated sugar

2 eggs

1. Lightly grease two baking sheets. Sift the flour, baking powder, and salt into a bowl and set aside.

2. In a separate bowl, beat the peanut butter, butter, and vanilla extract until smooth. Beat in the sugars for 1 minute, then beat in the eggs one at a time. Stir in the flour mixture in two batches and mix to form a dough.

3. Shape the dough into a ball, then wrap the ball in plastic wrap and chill in the refrigerator for at least 2 hours.

4. Preheat the oven to 350°F.

5. Unwrap the dough, roll into 1½-inch balls, and place them on the prepared baking sheets, spaced well apart. Use a fork to flatten each ball, making a crisscross pattern.

6. Bake in the preheated oven for 15 minutes, or until golden. Let cool on the baking sheets for a few minutes, then transfer to a wire rack to cool completely.

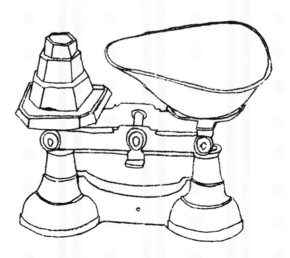

2

3

5

Refrigerator Cookies

makes 56

ingredients

2⅔ cups all-purpose flour

2 tablespoons unsweetened
cocoa powder

½ teaspoon baking soda

1 teaspoon ground ginger

½ teaspoon ground cinnamon

½ cup molasses

¼ cup boiling water

1 stick unsalted butter,
softened

¼ superfine sugar or
granulated sugar

confectioners' sugar,
for dusting

1. Sift the flour, cocoa powder, baking soda, ginger, and cinnamon into a bowl, then set aside. Mix the molasses with the water and set aside.

2. Put the butter into a large bowl and beat with an electric mixer until creamy. Slowly add the superfine or granulated sugar and continue beating until light and fluffy. Gradually add the flour mixture, alternating it with the molasses mixture to form a soft dough.

3. Scrape equal amounts of the dough onto two pieces of plastic wrap and roll into logs, each about 7½ inches long and 1½ inches thick. Wrap in the plastic wrap and put the dough logs in the refrigerator for 2 hours, then transfer to the freezer for at least 2 hours and up to 2 months.

4. When ready to bake, preheat the oven to 350°F. Depending on how many cookies you are baking, line one or two baking sheets with parchment paper. Unwrap the dough logs, trim the ends, and cut off as many ¼-inch slices as you require. Rewrap any unused dough and return to the freezer for another time.

5. Place the dough slices on the prepared baking sheet and bake in the preheated oven for 12 minutes. Let cool on the baking sheet for a few minutes, then transfer to a wire rack. Dust with confectioners' sugar and let cool completely.

1

2

3

Gingersnaps

makes 30

ingredients

2¾ cups all-purpose flour

pinch of salt

1 cup superfine sugar or
granulated sugar

1 tablespoon ground ginger

2¾ teaspoons baking powder

1 teaspoon baking soda

1 stick unsalted butter,
plus extra for greasing

⅓ cup light corn syrup

1 egg, beaten

1 teaspoon grated orange zest

1. Preheat the oven to 325°F. Lightly grease two or three baking sheets.

2. Sift the flour, salt, sugar, ginger, baking powder, and baking soda into a large bowl and set aside.

3. Heat the butter and light corn syrup in a saucepan over low heat until the butter has melted. Remove the pan from the heat and let cool slightly, then pour the contents onto the dry ingredients.

4. Add the egg and orange zest and mix thoroughly with a wooden spoon to form a dough. Using your hands, carefully shape the dough into 30 equal balls. Place the balls on the prepared baking sheets, spaced well apart, then flatten them slightly with your fingers.

5. Bake in the preheated oven for 15–20 minutes. Let cool on the baking sheets for a few minutes, then transfer to wire racks to cool completely.

2

3

4

Double Chocolate Whoopie Pies

makes 12

ingredients

1⅔ cups all-purpose flour

1½ teaspoons baking soda

¼ cup unsweetened cocoa powder

large pinch of salt

6 tablespoons unsalted butter, softened

⅓ cup vegetable shortening

¾ cup firmly packed light brown sugar

3 tablespoons finely grated semisweet chocolate

1 extra-large egg, beaten

½ cup milk

¼ cup chocolate sprinkles

white chocolate filling

6 ounces white chocolate, broken into pieces

2 tablespoons milk

1¼ cups heavy cream

1. Preheat the oven to 350°F. Line two or three large baking sheets with parchment paper.

2. Sift the flour, baking soda, cocoa powder, and salt into a large bowl and set aside.

3. Place the butter, vegetable shortening, sugar, and grated chocolate in a separate large bowl and beat with an electric mixer until pale and fluffy. Beat in the egg, followed by half the flour mixture, then the milk. Stir in the rest of the flour mixture and mix until thoroughly incorporated.

4. Pipe or spoon 24 mounds of the dough onto the prepared baking sheets, spaced well apart. Bake in the preheated oven for 10–12 minutes, or until risen and just firm to the touch. Let cool on the baking sheets for a few minutes, then transfer to wire racks to cool completely.

5. To make the filling, put the white chocolate and milk into a heatproof bowl set over a saucepan of gently simmering water. Heat until the chocolate has melted, stirring occasionally. Remove from the heat and let cool for 30 minutes. Using an electric mixer, whip the cream until holding firm peaks. Fold in the cooled melted chocolate. Cover and chill in the refrigerator for 30–45 minutes, or until firm enough to spread.

6. To assemble, spread or pipe the chocolate filling on the flat side of half the whoopie pies. Top with the remaining whoopie pies. Spread out the chocolate sprinkles on a plate and gently roll the edges of each whoopie pie in the sprinkles to lightly coat.

hints & tips

For extra rich and chocolaty whoopie pies, use semisweet chocolate for the filling.

Jelly Rings

makes 15

ingredients

2 sticks unsalted butter, softened

¾ cup superfine sugar or granulated sugar, plus extra for sprinkling

1 egg yolk, lightly beaten

2 teaspoons vanilla extract

2¼ cups all-purpose flour

pinch of salt

1 egg white, lightly beaten

filling

4 tablespoons unsalted butter, softened

¾ cup confectioners' sugar

⅓ cup strawberry or raspberry jelly

1. Put the butter and superfine or granulated sugar into a bowl and mix well, then beat in the egg yolk and vanilla extract. Sift the flour and salt into the mixture and mix to form a dough.

2. Halve the dough and shape into two balls, then wrap in plastic wrap and chill in the refrigerator for 30–60 minutes.

3. Preheat the oven to 375°F. Line two baking sheets with parchment paper.

4. Unwrap the dough and roll out between two sheets of parchment paper. Stamp out cookies with a 2¾-inch fluted, round cutter and put half of them on one of the prepared baking sheets, spaced well apart. Using a 1½-inch plain, round cutter, stamp out the centers of the remaining cookies and remove. Put the cookie rings on the other baking sheet, spaced well apart.

5. Bake in the preheated oven for 7 minutes, then brush the cookie rings with the beaten egg white and sprinkle with superfine or granulated sugar. Bake for an additional 5–8 minutes, until light golden brown. Let cool on the baking sheets for a few minutes, then transfer to wire racks to cool completely.

6. To make the filling, beat the butter and confectioners' sugar in a bowl. Spread the buttercream over the whole cookies and top with the jelly. Place the cookie rings on top and press together.

hints & tips

Add grated lemon zest to
the buttercream and replace
the jelly with lemon curd.

Cappuccino Cookies

makes 30

ingredients

2 envelopes instant
cappuccino

1 tablespoon hot water

2 sticks unsalted butter,
softened

¾ cup superfine sugar or
granulated sugar

1 egg yolk, lightly beaten

2¼ cups all-purpose flour

pinch of salt

topping

6 ounces white chocolate,
broken into pieces

unsweetened cocoa powder,
for dusting

1. Empty the cappuccino into a small bowl and stir in the hot, but not boiling, water to make a paste. Put the butter and sugar into a bowl and beat together until pale and creamy, then beat in the egg yolk and cappuccino paste. Sift the flour and salt into the mixture and stir until thoroughly combined.

2. Halve the dough and shape into two balls, then wrap in plastic wrap and chill in the refrigerator for 30–60 minutes.

3. Preheat the oven to 375°F. Line two baking sheets with parchment paper.

4. Unwrap the dough and roll out between two sheets of parchment paper. Stamp out circles with a 2½-inch round cutter and put them on the prepared baking sheets, spaced well apart.

5. Bake in the preheated oven for 10–12 minutes, or until golden brown. Let cool on the baking sheets for a few minutes, then transfer to wire racks to cool completely.

6. When the cookies are cool, place the wire racks over a sheet of parchment paper. Put the chocolate into a heatproof bowl set over a saucepan of gently simmering water and stir until melted. Remove from the heat and let cool slightly. Spoon the chocolate over the cookies, gently tap the wire racks to level the surface, and let set. Lightly dust with cocoa before serving.

1

2

4

Traditional Shortbread

makes 8

ingredients

1⅓ cups all-purpose flour,
plus extra for dusting

pinch of salt

¼ cup superfine sugar or
granulated sugar, plus extra
for sprinkling

1 stick unsalted butter,
cut into small pieces

1. Preheat the oven to 300°F. Line a baking sheet with parchment paper.

2. Put the flour, salt, and sugar into a large bowl and mix together. Add the butter and rub it into the dry ingredients with your fingertips. Continue to work the mixture until it forms a soft dough. Make sure you do not overwork the shortbread or it will be tough.

3. Roll out the dough on a lightly floured surface to form an 8-inch circle. Transfer to the prepared baking sheet and pinch the edges to form a scalloped pattern. Using a knife, mark the dough into eight pieces and prick all over with a fork.

4. Bake in the preheated oven for 45–50 minutes, or until the shortbread is firm and just a pale golden brown. Let cool on the baking sheet for a few minutes, then sprinkle with sugar. Cut into portions and transfer to a wire rack to cool completely.

2

3

4

Thumbprint Cookies

makes 36

ingredients

1 stick unsalted butter, softened

⅔ cup superfine sugar or granulated sugar

1 extra-large egg, separated

1 teaspoon vanilla extract

1⅓ cups all-purpose flour

pinch of salt

¼ cup ground almonds (almond meal)

⅓ cup raspberry jelly or preserves

1. Preheat the oven to 350°F. Line two large baking sheets with parchment paper.

2. Put the butter and ½ cup of the sugar into a large bowl and beat until light and fluffy. Add the egg yolk and vanilla extract and beat well to combine. Sift in the flour and salt and mix well.

3. Mix together the remaining sugar and the ground almonds and spread out on a plate. Lightly whisk the egg white in a separate bowl.

4. Roll walnut-size pieces of the dough into balls, then dip each ball into the egg white and roll in the almond sugar. Place the balls on the prepared baking sheets, spaced well apart, and make a deep indentation in the center of each one with a thumb.

5. Bake in the preheated oven for 10 minutes. Remove from the oven, press down again on each indentation, and fill it with jelly. Bake for an additional 10–12 minutes, or until the cookies are golden brown. Let cool on the baking sheets for a few minutes, then transfer to wire racks to cool completely.

hints & tips

For a delicious variation,
replace the raspberry jelly
with lemon curd.

Black & White Cookies

makes 20

ingredients

1 stick unsalted butter,
softened, plus extra
for greasing

1 teaspoon vanilla extract

¾ cup superfine sugar or
granulated sugar

2 eggs, beaten

2⅓ cups all-purpose flour

½ teaspoon baking powder

1 cup milk

topping

1¾ cups confectioners' sugar

½ cup heavy cream

a few drops of vanilla extract

3 ounces semisweet chocolate,
broken into pieces

1. Preheat the oven to 375°F. Lightly grease three baking sheets.

2. Place the butter, vanilla extract, and superfine or granulated sugar in a large bowl. Beat the mixture with an electric mixer until light and fluffy, then beat in the eggs one at a time.

3. Sift the flour and baking powder into a separate bowl, then gradually fold the flour mixture into the creamed mixture, loosening with the milk as you work until both are used up and the mixture is of dropping consistency.

4. Drop tablespoonfuls of the dough onto the prepared baking sheets, spaced well apart.

5. Bake in the preheated oven for 15 minutes, or until the cookies are turning golden at the edges and are light to the touch. Let cool on the baking sheets for a few minutes, then transfer to wire racks to cool completely.

6. Put the confectioners' sugar into a bowl and mix in half the cream and the vanilla extract. The consistency should be thick but spreadable. Using a spatula, spread half of each cookie with the white icing.

7. Place the chocolate in a heatproof bowl over a saucepan of gently simmering water and stir until melted. Remove from the heat and stir in the remaining cream. Spread the dark icing over the uncoated cookie halves and let set.

Melting Moments

makes 32

ingredients

3 sticks unsalted butter, softened
⅔ cup confectioners' sugar
½ teaspoon vanilla extract
2⅓ cups all-purpose flour
⅓ cup cornstarch

1. Preheat the oven to 350°F. Line two large baking sheets with parchment paper.

2. Put the butter and confectioners' sugar into a large bowl and beat together until light and fluffy, then beat in the vanilla extract. Sift in the flour and cornstarch and mix thoroughly.

3. Spoon the dough into a pastry bag fitted with a large star tip. Pipe rosette shapes onto the prepared baking sheets, spaced well apart.

4. Bake in the preheated oven for 15–20 minutes, or until golden brown. Let cool completely on the baking sheets.

hints & tips
Make these cookies extra
special by dipping them
in melted chocolate.

47

Pistachio Biscotti

makes 30

ingredients

2 sticks unsalted butter, softened

¾ cup superfine sugar or granulated sugar

finely grated zest of 1 lemon

1 egg yolk, lightly beaten

2 teaspoons brandy

2¼ cups all-purpose flour

pinch of salt

¾ cup pistachio nuts

confectioners' sugar, for dusting

1. Put the butter, superfine or granulated sugar, and lemon zest into a bowl and mix well with a wooden spoon, then beat in the egg yolk and brandy. Sift the flour and salt into the mixture and stir in the pistachio nuts until thoroughly combined.

2. Shape the dough into a log, flatten slightly, wrap it in plastic wrap, and chill in the refrigerator for 30–60 minutes.

3. Preheat the oven to 375°F. Line two baking sheets with parchment paper.

4. Unwrap the log and cut it slightly on the diagonal into ¼-inch slices with a sharp, serrated knife. Place the slices on the prepared baking sheets, spaced well apart.

5. Bake in the preheated oven for 10 minutes, or until golden brown. Let cool on the baking sheets for a few minutes, then transfer to wire racks to cool completely. Dust with confectioners' sugar before serving.

Snickerdoodles

makes 40

ingredients

2 sticks unsalted butter, softened

¾ cup superfine sugar or granulated sugar

2 extra-large eggs, lightly beaten

1 teaspoon vanilla extract

3¼ cups all-purpose flour

1 teaspoon baking soda

½ teaspoon grated nutmeg

pinch of salt

½ cup finely chopped pecans

cinnamon coating

1 tablespoon granulated sugar

2 tablespoons ground cinnamon

1. Put the butter and sugar into a bowl and mix well with a wooden spoon, then beat in the eggs and vanilla extract. Sift the flour, baking soda, nutmeg, and salt into the mixture, add the pecans, and stir until thoroughly combined.

2. Shape the dough into a ball, wrap in plastic wrap, and chill in the refrigerator for 30–60 minutes.

3. Preheat the oven to 375°F. Line two or three baking sheets with parchment paper.

4. To make the cinnamon coating, mix together the sugar and cinnamon in a shallow dish. Scoop up tablespoons of the cookie dough and roll into balls. Roll each ball in the cinnamon mixture to coat and place on the prepared baking sheets, spaced well apart.

5. Bake in the preheated oven for 10–12 minutes, until golden brown. Let cool on the baking sheets for a few minutes, then transfer to wire racks to cool completely.

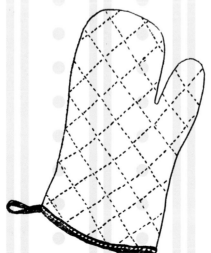

1 2 4

CHAPTER 2
SOFT & CHEWY

Double Chocolate & Cherry Cookies

makes 30

ingredients

2 sticks unsalted butter, softened

¾ cup superfine sugar or granulated sugar

1 egg yolk, lightly beaten

2 teaspoons vanilla extract

2 cups all-purpose flour

¼ cup unsweetned cocoa powder

pinch of salt

12 ounces semisweet chocolate, chopped

⅓ cup dried sour cherries

1. Preheat the oven to 375°F. Line two baking sheets with parchment paper.

2. Put the butter and sugar into a bowl and mix well with a wooden spoon, then beat in the egg yolk and vanilla extract. Sift the flour, cocoa, and salt into the mixture, add the chopped chocolate and sour cherries, and stir until thoroughly combined.

3. Scoop up tablespoons of the dough and shape into balls. Put them on the prepared baking sheets, spaced well apart, and flatten slightly.

4. Bake in the preheated oven for 12–15 minutes. Let cool on the baking sheets for a few minutes, then transfer to wire racks to cool completely.

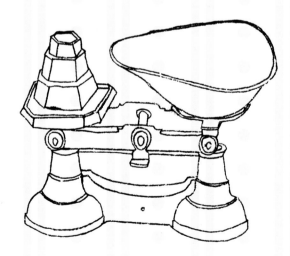

hints & tips
Use a semisweet chocolate with a high percentage of cocoa solids for this recipe.

Soft & Chewy
CHAPTER 2

55

Pumpkin Pie Cookies

makes 20

ingredients

1 stick unsalted butter, softened

½ cup superfine sugar or granulated sugar

½ cup firmly packed light brown sugar

1 egg, lightly beaten

½ teaspoon vanilla extract

⅔ cup canned pumpkin puree

2 cups all-purpose flour

¼ teaspoon salt

1½ teaspoons ground cinnamon

¼ teaspoon each ground ginger, ground cloves, and freshly grated nutmeg

maple glaze

1 cup confectioners' sugar

1 tablespoon maple syrup

1–2 tablespoons warm water

1. Preheat the oven to 350°F. Line three baking sheets with parchment paper.

2. Place the butter and sugars in a large bowl and beat together until pale and fluffy. Gradually beat in the egg, then stir in the vanilla extract and pumpkin puree. Sift in the flour, salt, and spices and stir until thoroughly combined.

3. Place 20 tablespoonfuls of the dough onto the prepared baking sheets and spread each out to a 2½-inch circle with the back of a spoon.

4. Bake in the preheated oven for 15–20 minutes, or until golden and firm to the touch. Let cool on the baking sheets for a few minutes, then transfer to wire racks to cool completely.

5. To make the glaze, sift the confectioners' sugar into a bowl. Add the maple syrup and 1 tablespoon of warm water and beat together until smooth. Add a little extra water, if needed, to create a fairly runny consistency. Spoon the glaze over the pumpkin cookies and let set.

2 3 5

Chewy Ginger & Molasses Cookies

makes 28

ingredients

1 stick unsalted butter, plus extra for greasing

¼ cup molasses

2¾ cups all-purpose flour

2¾ teaspoons baking powder

1 teaspoon baking soda

2 teaspoons ground ginger

1 teaspoon ground cinnamon

¾ cup firmly packed light brown sugar

1 extra-large egg, beaten

2 tablespoons raw brown sugar

1. Preheat the oven to 325°F. Lightly grease two or three large baking sheets.

2. Place the butter and molasses in a small saucepan and heat gently until the butter has melted. Let cool for 10 minutes.

3. Sift the flour, baking powder, baking soda, and spices into a large bowl. Stir in the brown sugar and make a well in the center. Pour in the cooled butter mixture and the egg and mix thoroughly to form a crumbly dough. Use your hands to gather the dough together.

4. Shape the dough into 28 walnut-size balls. Place on the prepared baking sheets, spaced well apart, and flatten each one slightly. Sprinkle the raw brown sugar over the top.

5. Bake in the preheated oven for 10–12 minutes, or until just set and the surfaces are cracked. Let cool on the baking sheets for a few minutes, then transfer to wire racks to cool completely.

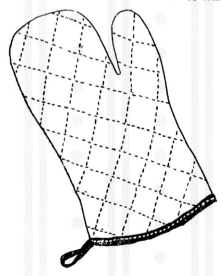

2

3

4

White Chocolate & Macadamia Nut Cookies

makes 16

ingredients

1 stick unsalted butter, softened, plus extra for greasing

½ cup firmly packed light brown sugar

1 tablespoon light corn syrup

1⅓ cups all-purpose flour

1¼ teaspoons baking powder

⅓ cup coarsely chopped macadamia nuts

2 ounces white chocolate, cut into chunks

1. Preheat the oven to 350°F. Lightly grease two large baking sheets.

2. Put the butter and sugar into a bowl and beat until pale and creamy, then beat in the corn syrup. Sift in the flour and baking powder, add the nuts, and mix to form a coarse dough.

3. Shape the dough into 16 equal balls and place on the prepared baking sheets, spaced well apart. Slightly flatten each ball and top with the chocolate chunks, pressing them lightly into the dough.

4. Bake in the preheated oven for 12–14 minutes, or until just set and pale golden. Let cool on the baking sheets for a few minutes, then transfer to wire racks to cool completely.

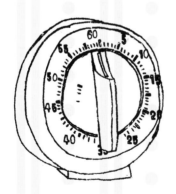

2

3

4

Banana Toffee Cookies

makes 16

ingredients

1 stick unsalted butter,
softened

½ cup firmly packed light
brown sugar

1 tablespoon maple syrup

1 small banana, peeled
and mashed

1¾ cups all-purpose flour

1¾ teaspoons baking powder

2 ounces hard toffees,
coarsely crushed

1. Preheat the oven to 350°F. Line two large baking sheets with parchment paper.

2. Put the butter, sugar, and maple syrup into a large bowl and beat until pale and creamy. Stir in the mashed banana. Sift in the flour and baking powder, and mix to form a soft, slightly sticky dough. Stir in the crushed toffees.

3. Shape the dough into 16 walnut-size balls. Place on the prepared baking sheets, spaced well apart, and flatten each one slightly.

4. Bake in the preheated oven for 11–12 minutes, or until pale golden. Let cool on the baking sheets for a few minutes, then transfer to wire racks to cool completely.

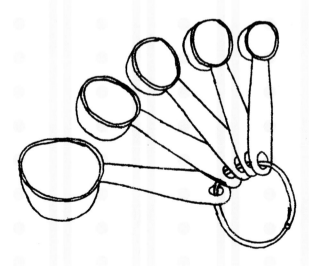

2

3

4

Chocolate Chip & Cinnamon Cookies

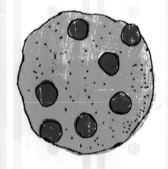

makes 30

ingredients

2 sticks unsalted butter, softened

¾ cup superfine sugar or granulated sugar

1 egg yolk, lightly beaten

2 teaspoons orange extract

2¼ cups all-purpose flour

pinch of salt

½ cup semisweet chocolate chips

cinnamon coating

1½ tablespoons superfine sugar or granulated sugar

1½ tablespoons ground cinnamon

1. Preheat the oven to 375°F. Line two baking sheets with parchment paper.

2. Put the butter and sugar into a bowl and mix well with a wooden spoon, then beat in the egg yolk and orange extract. Sift the flour and salt into the mixture, add the chocolate chips, and stir until thoroughly combined.

3. For the cinnamon coating, mix together the superfine or granulated sugar and cinnamon in a shallow dish.

4. Scoop up tablespoons of the cookie dough and roll them into balls, then roll them in the cinnamon mixture to coat. Put them on the prepared baking sheets, spaced well apart.

5. Bake in the preheated oven for 12–15 minutes. Let cool on the baking sheets for a few minutes, then transfer to wire racks to cool completely.

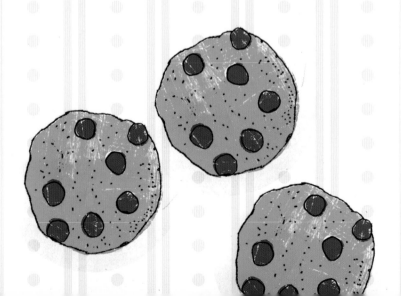

2

2

4

Mocha Walnut Cookies

makes 16

ingredients

1 stick unsalted butter, softened, plus extra for greasing

½ cup firmly packed light brown sugar

⅓ cup superfine sugar or granulated sugar

1 teaspoon vanilla extract

1 tablespoon instant coffee granules, dissolved in 1 tablespoon hot water

1 egg

1⅓ cups all-purpose flour

½ teaspoon baking powder

¼ teaspoon baking soda

⅓ cup milk chocolate chips

½ cup coarsely chopped walnuts

1. Preheat the oven to 350°F. Lightly grease two large baking sheets.

2. Put the butter and sugars into a large bowl and beat together until light and fluffy. Put the vanilla extract, coffee, and egg into a separate bowl and whisk together. Gradually add the coffee mixture to the creamed mixture, beating until fluffy. Sift the flour, baking powder, and baking soda into the mixture and fold in carefully. Fold in the chocolate chips and walnuts.

3. Spoon tablespoonfuls of the dough onto the prepared baking sheets, spaced well apart.

4. Bake in the preheated oven for 10–15 minutes, or until crisp on the outside but soft inside. Let cool on the baking sheets for a few minutes, then transfer to wire racks to cool completely.

hints & tips

Try semisweet or white chocolate chips instead of the milk chocolate chips.

Midnight Cookies

makes 25

ingredients

1 stick unsalted butter, softened

¾ cup superfine sugar or granulated sugar

1 egg, lightly beaten

½ teaspoon vanilla extract

1 cup all-purpose flour

⅓ cup unsweetened cocoa powder

½ teaspoon baking soda

melted semisweet chocolate, to serve (optional)

1. Preheat the oven to 350°F. Line several large baking sheets with parchment paper.

2. Put the butter and sugar into a large bowl and beat together until light and fluffy. Add the egg and vanilla extract and mix until smooth. Sift in the flour, cocoa, and baking soda and beat until well mixed.

3. With dampened hands, roll walnut-size pieces of the dough into smooth balls. Place on the prepared baking sheets, spaced well apart.

4. Bake in the preheated oven for 10–12 minutes, or until set. Let cool on the baking sheets for a few minutes, then transfer to wire racks to cool completely. If desired, serve with a small bowl of melted semisweet chocolate for dipping.

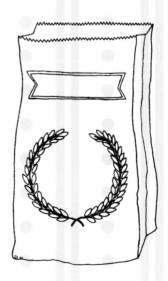

2

3

3

Chocolate & Hazelnut Drops

makes 30

ingredients

2 sticks unsalted butter, softened

¾ cup superfine sugar or granulated sugar

1 egg yolk, lightly beaten

2 teaspoons vanilla extract

1¾ cups all-purpose flour

½ cup unsweetened cocoa powder

pinch of salt

½ cup ground hazelnuts

¼ cup semisweet chocolate chips

¼ cup chocolate hazelnut spread

1. Preheat the oven to 375°F. Line two baking sheets with parchment paper.

2. Put the butter and sugar into a bowl and mix well with a wooden spoon, then beat in the egg yolk and vanilla extract. Sift the flour, cocoa, and salt into the mixture, then add the ground hazelnuts and chocolate chips and stir until thoroughly combined.

3. Scoop up tablespoonfuls of the batter and shape into balls with your hands, then put them on the prepared baking sheets, spaced well apart. Use the dampened handle of a wooden spoon to make a hollow in the center of each ball.

4. Bake in the preheated oven for 12–15 minutes. Let cool on the baking sheets for a few minutes, then transfer to wire racks to cool completely. When the cookies are cold, fill the hollows with the chocolate hazelnut spread.

hints & tips

For a change, fill with peanut butter instead of the chocolate hazelnut spread.

Soft & Chewy
CHAPTER 2

Coconut & Cranberry Cookies

makes 30

ingredients

2 sticks unsalted butter, softened

¾ cup superfine sugar or granulated sugar

1 egg yolk

2 teaspoons vanilla extract

2¼ cups all-purpose flour

pinch of salt

½ cup shredded dried coconut

½ cup dried cranberries

1. Preheat the oven to 375°F. Line several baking sheets with parchment paper.

2. Put the butter and sugar into a bowl and beat together until pale and creamy, then beat in the egg yolk and vanilla extract. Sift the flour and salt into the mixture, add the coconut and cranberries, and stir until thoroughly combined.

3. Scoop up tablespoonfuls of the dough and place in mounds on the prepared baking sheets, spaced well apart.

4. Bake in the preheated oven for 12–15 minutes, or until golden brown. Let cool on the baking sheets for a few minutes, then transfer to wire racks to cool completely.

2

2

3

Banana & Raisin Cookies

makes 30

ingredients

3 tablespoons raisins

½ cup orange juice or rum

2 sticks unsalted butter,
softened

¾ cup superfine sugar or
granulated sugar

1 egg yolk, lightly beaten

2¼ cups all-purpose flour

pinch of salt

¾ cup dried bananas,
finely chopped

1. Put the raisins into a bowl, pour in the orange juice or rum, and let soak for 30 minutes. Drain the raisins, reserving any remaining liquid.

2. Preheat the oven to 375°F. Line two baking sheets with parchment paper.

3. Put the butter and sugar into a bowl and mix well with a wooden spoon, then beat in the egg yolk and 2 teaspoons of the reserved liquid. Sift the flour and salt into the mixture, add the raisins and dried bananas, and stir until thoroughly combined.

4. Put tablespoonfuls of the dough into mounds on the prepared baking sheets, spaced well apart, then flatten them gently.

5. Bake in the preheated oven for 12–15 minutes, until golden. Let cool on the baking sheets for a few minutes, then transfer to wire racks to cool completely.

hints & tips

For a tropical taste, replace the raisins with finely chopped dried mango.

Apple & Oatmeal Cookies

makes 26

ingredients

2 large apples,
peeled and cored

1 teaspoon lemon juice

2 sticks unsalted butter,
softened, plus extra
for greasing

½ cup firmly packed light
brown sugar

½ cup superfine sugar or
granulated sugar

1 egg, beaten

1¾ cups all-purpose flour

1¾ teaspoons baking powder

1⅔ cups rolled oats

½ cup raisins

1. Preheat the oven to 350°F. Grease three large baking sheets. Finely dice the apples and toss in the lemon juice.

2. Put the butter and sugars into a bowl and beat together until creamy. Gradually beat in the egg. Sift in the flour and baking powder and add the oats, raisins, and apples. Mix until thoroughly combined.

3. Place tablespoonfuls of the batter on the prepared baking sheets, spaced well apart.

4. Bake in the preheated oven for 12–15 minutes, or until golden around the edges. Let cool on the baking sheets for a few minutes, then transfer to wire racks to cool completely.

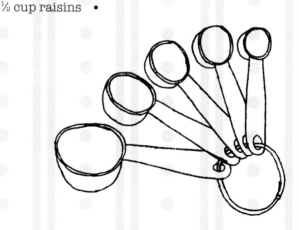

Pecan Brownie Cookies

makes 18

ingredients

6 ounces semisweet chocolate, broken into pieces

6 tablespoons unsalted butter, softened

¾ cup firmly packed light brown sugar

2 eggs, lightly beaten

1 teaspoon vanilla extract

1⅓ cups all-purpose flour

½ teaspoon baking powder

¾ cup chopped pecans

1. Preheat the oven to 375°F. Line two large baking sheets with parchment paper.

2. Place the chocolate in a heatproof bowl set over a saucepan of gently simmering water and stir until melted. Remove from the heat and let cool for 10 minutes.

3. Put the butter and sugar into a large bowl and beat together until pale and creamy. Gradually beat in the eggs, then stir in the vanilla extract and cooled melted chocolate.

4. Sift in the flour and baking powder and add ½ cup of the chopped pecans. Stir until thoroughly combined.

5. Drop 18 tablespoonfuls of the dough onto the prepared baking sheets, spaced well apart. Flatten each one slightly with the back of the spoon and top with the remaining chopped pecans.

6. Bake for 11–12 minutes, or until just firm to the touch. Let cool on the baking sheets for a few minutes, then transfer to wire racks to cool completely.

hints & tips

If you desire, drizzle the cooled cookies with melted white chocolate.

German Lebkuchen

makes 60

ingredients

3 eggs

1 cup superfine sugar or granulated sugar

⅓ cup all-purpose flour

2 teaspoons unsweetened cocoa powder

1 teaspoon ground cinnamon

½ teaspoon ground cardamom

¼ teaspoon ground cloves

¼ teaspoon ground nutmeg

1¾ cups ground almonds (almond meal)

¼ cup finely chopped candied peel

topping

4 ounces semisweet chocolate, broken into pieces

4 ounces white chocolate, broken into pieces

large sugar crystals, to decorate (optional)

1. Preheat the oven to 350°F. Line several large baking sheets with parchment paper.

2. Place the eggs and sugar in a heatproof bowl set over a saucepan of gently simmering water and, using an electric mixer, beat until thick and foamy. Remove the bowl from the pan and continue to beat for 2 minutes.

3. Sift the flour, cocoa, cinnamon, cardamom, cloves, and nutmeg into the bowl and stir in with the ground almonds and candied peel.

4. Drop tablespoonfuls of the dough onto the prepared baking sheets, spreading them gently into smooth mounds.

5. Bake in the preheated oven for 15–20 minutes, or until light brown and slightly soft to the touch. Let cool on the baking sheets for a few minutes, then transfer to wire racks to cool completely.

6. Put the semisweet and white chocolate into separate heatproof bowls, each set over a saucepan of gently simmering water, and stir until melted. Remove from the heat and let cool slightly.

7. Spoon the melted semisweet chocolate over half the cookies and the melted white chocolate over the rest and place on a wire rack set over a sheet of parchment paper. Sprinkle with sugar crystals, if desired, and let set.

Peach Daiquiri Cookies

makes 30

ingredients

2 sticks unsalted butter,
softened

¾ cup superfine sugar or
granulated sugar

finely grated zest of 1 lime

1 egg yolk, lightly beaten

2 teaspoons white rum

2¼ cups all-purpose flour

pinch of salt

1 cup chopped dried peach

white rum glaze

1¼ cups confectioners' sugar

1-2 tablespoons white rum

1. Preheat the oven to 375°F. Line two baking sheets with parchment paper.

2. Put the butter, superfine or granulated sugar, and lime zest into a bowl and mix well with a wooden spoon, then beat in the egg yolk and rum. Sift the flour and salt into the mixture, add the peach, and stir until thoroughly combined.

3. Scoop up tablespoonfuls of the dough and put them on the prepared baking sheets, spaced well apart, then flatten gently.

4. Bake in the preheated oven for 10–15 minutes, until light golden brown. Let cool on the baking sheets for a few minutes, then transfer to wire racks to cool completely.

5. Sift the confectioners' sugar into a bowl and stir in enough of the rum to give the mixture the consistency of thick cream. Leaving the cookies on the racks, drizzle the glaze over them with a teaspoon and let set.

hints & tips

To add a fruity flavor to the glaze, use peach juice instead of the rum.

Brown Sugar
Blueberry Cookies

makes 18

ingredients

1 stick unsalted butter, softened

¾ cup light brown sugar

1 egg, lightly beaten

1 teaspoon vanilla extract

1¾ cups all-purpose flour

pinch of salt

¾ teaspoon baking powder

1 teaspoon ground cinnamon

2 tablespoons milk

1 cup fresh blueberries

1. Preheat the oven to 375°F. Line three baking sheets with parchment paper.

2. Put the butter and sugar into a large bowl and, using an electric mixer, beat together until smooth and creamy. Gradually beat in the egg and the vanilla extract.

3. Sift in the flour, salt, baking powder, and cinnamon and add the milk. Mix thoroughly with a wooden spoon or spatula to make a soft, sticky dough. Fold in the blueberries.

4. Place 18 tablespoonfuls of the dough onto the prepared baking sheets, spaced well apart.

5. Bake in the preheated oven for 11–12 minutes, or until puffy and pale golden. Let cool on the baking sheets for a few minutes, then transfer to wire racks to cool completely.

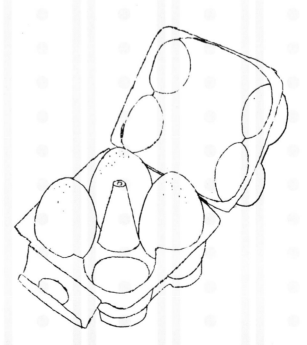

2

3

5

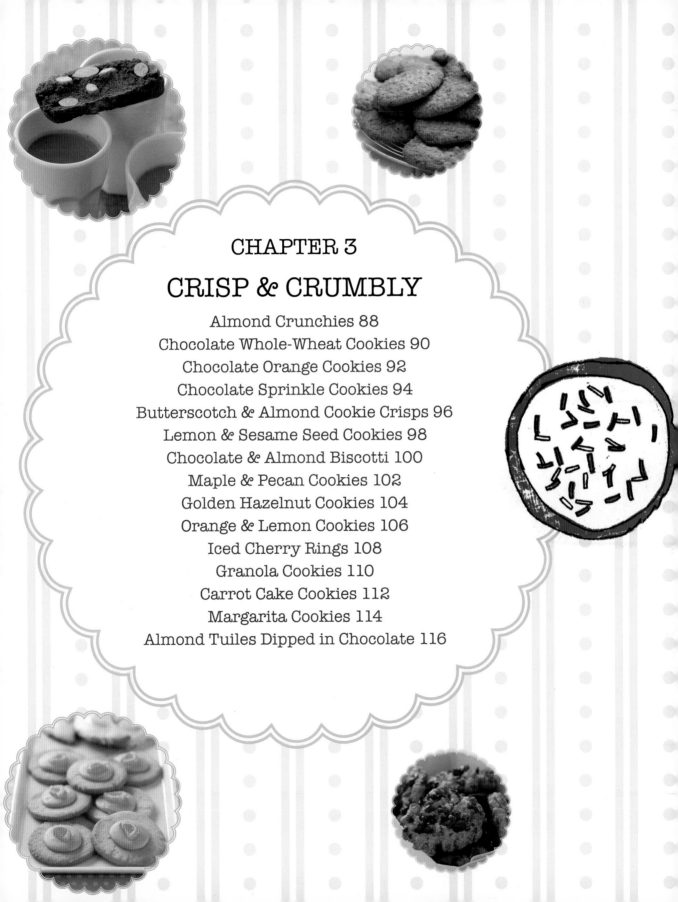

CHAPTER 3

CRISP & CRUMBLY

Almond Crunchies

makes 50

ingredients

2 sticks unsalted butter, softened

¾ cup superfine sugar or granulated sugar

1 egg yolk, lightly beaten

½ teaspoon almond extract

1¾ cups all-purpose flour

pinch of salt

1½ cups blanched almonds, chopped

1. Put the butter and sugar into a bowl and mix well with a wooden spoon, then beat in the egg yolk and almond extract. Sift the flour and salt into the mixture, add the almonds, and stir until thoroughly combined.

2. Halve the dough and shape into two balls, then wrap in plastic wrap and chill in the refrigerator for 30-60 minutes.

3. Preheat the oven to 375°F. Line two or three baking sheets with parchment paper.

4. Unwrap the dough, shape into 50 small balls, and flatten them slightly between the palms of your hands. Put on the prepared baking sheets, spaced well apart.

5. Bake in the preheated oven for 15-20 minutes, until golden brown. Let cool on the baking sheets for a few minutes, then transfer to wire racks to cool completely.

hints & tips

These cookies are an
excellent accompaniment to
a creamy dessert.

Crisp & Crumbly
CHAPTER 3

Chocolate Whole-Wheat Cookies

makes 20

ingredients

6 tablespoons unsalted butter

⅔ cup raw brown sugar

1 egg

1 tablespoon wheat germ

1¼ cup whole-wheat flour

⅔ cup white all-purpose flour

1¾ teaspoons baking powder

4 ounces semisweet chocolate, broken into pieces

1. Preheat the oven to 350°F. Line two or three baking sheets with parchment paper.

2. Put the butter and sugar into a large bowl and beat together until light and fluffy. Add the egg and beat well. Stir in the wheat germ, flours, and baking powder, then bring the mixture together with your hands.

3. Roll rounded teaspoonfuls of the dough into balls. Place them on the prepared baking sheets, spaced well apart, then flatten slightly.

4. Bake in the preheated oven for 15–20 minutes, or until golden brown. Let cool on the baking sheets for a few minutes, then transfer to wire racks to cool completely.

5. Put the chocolate into a heatproof bowl set over a saucepan of gently simmering water and stir until melted. Dip each cookie in the chocolate to cover the flat side and a little way around the edges. Let any excess chocolate drip back into the bowl. Place the cookies on a sheet of parchment paper in a cool place and let set.

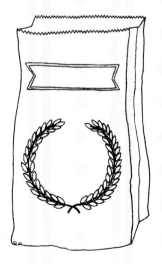

2

3

5

Chocolate Orange Cookies

makes 30

ingredients

6 tablespoons unsalted butter, softened

¼ cup superfine sugar or granulated sugar

1 egg

1 tablespoon milk

2¼ cups all-purpose flour, plus extra for dusting

2 tablespoons unsweetened cocoa powder

topping

1⅓ cups confectioners' sugar

2–3 tablespoons orange juice

4 ounces semisweet chocolate, broken into pieces

1. Preheat the oven to 350°F. Line two large baking sheets with parchment paper.

2. Put the butter and superfine or granulated sugar into a large bowl and beat together until light and fluffy. Beat in the egg and milk until thoroughly combined. Sift the flour and cocoa into the bowl and gradually mix together to form a soft dough.

3. Roll out the dough on a lightly floured surface until about ¼ inch thick. Cut out circles with a 2-inch fluted, round cutter and transfer to the prepared baking sheets.

4. Bake in the preheated oven for 10–12 minutes, or until golden. Let cool on the baking sheets for a few minutes, then transfer to wire racks to cool completely and become crisp.

5. Sift the confectioners' sugar into a bowl and stir in enough of the orange juice to form a thin glaze that will coat the back of the spoon. Place a spoonful of the icing in the center of each cookie and let set.

6. Put the chocolate into a heatproof bowl set over a saucepan of gently simmering water and heat until melted. Let cool slightly, then spoon into a paper pastry bag and snip off the end. Drizzle the melted chocolate over the cookies and let set before serving.

3

5

6

Chocolate Sprinkle Cookies

makes 30

ingredients

2 sticks unsalted butter, softened

¾ cup superfine sugar or granulated sugar

1 egg yolk, lightly beaten

2 teaspoons vanilla extract

1¾ cups all-purpose flour, plus extra for dusting

½ cup unsweetened cocoa powder

pinch of salt

topping

8 ounces white chocolate, broken into pieces

⅓ cup chocolate sprinkles

1. Put the butter and sugar into a bowl and mix well with a wooden spoon, then beat in the egg yolk and vanilla extract. Sift the flour, cocoa, and salt into the mixture and stir until thoroughly combined.

2. Halve the dough and shape into two balls, then wrap in plastic wrap and chill in the refrigerator for 30–60 minutes.

3. Preheat the oven to 375°F. Line two baking sheets with parchment paper.

4. Unwrap the dough and roll out between two sheets of parchment paper to about ¼ inch thick. Stamp out 30 cookies with a 2½–2¾-inch fluted, round cutter. Put them on the prepared baking sheets, spaced well apart.

5. Bake in the preheated oven for 10–12 minutes. Let cool on the baking sheets for a few minutes, then transfer to wire racks to cool completely.

6. Put the chocolate into a heatproof bowl set over a saucepan of gently simmering water and stir until melted. Remove from the heat. Spread the melted chocolate over the cookies and let cool slightly, then sprinkle with the chocolate sprinkles. Let set.

hints & tips

Instead of using sprinkles, decorate with a swirl of melted semisweet chocolate.

Crisp & Crumbly
CHAPTER 3

hints & tips

Instead of using sprinkles, decorate with a swirl of melted semisweet chocolate.

Crisp & Crumbly
CHAPTER 3

Butterscotch & Almond Cookie Crisps

makes 18

ingredients

2 egg whites

½ cup firmly packed light brown sugar

½ teaspoon vanilla extract

4 tablespoons unsalted butter, melted and cooled

⅓ cup all-purpose flour

3 tablespoons slivered almonds

1. Preheat the oven to 350°F. Line three baking sheets with parchment paper.

2. Put the egg whites into a large bowl and, using a wire whisk, beat until frothy. Add the sugar and vanilla extract and whisk for 2–3 minutes. Whisk in the melted butter, then sift in the flour and mix thoroughly to make a smooth, thick batter.

3. Drop tablespoonfuls of the batter onto the prepared baking sheets, spaced well apart. Using the back of the spoon, spread each spoonful of batter to form a 3½-inch circle. Sprinkle with the slivered almonds.

4. Bake in the preheated oven for 8–10 minutes, or until the cookies are deep golden brown around the edges. Let cool on the baking sheets for a few minutes, then transfer to wire racks to cool completely.

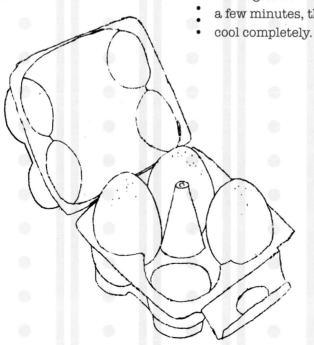

Crisp & Crumbly
CHAPTER 3

Lemon & Sesame Seed Cookies

makes 30

ingredients

2 tablespoons sesame seeds

2 sticks unsalted butter, softened

¾ cup superfine sugar or granulated sugar

1 tablespoon finely grated lemon zest

1 egg yolk, lightly beaten

2¼ cups all-purpose flour

pinch of salt

lemon glaze

1 cup confectioners' sugar

a few drops of lemon extract

1 tablespoon hot water

1. Dry-fry the sesame seeds in a heavy skillet over low heat, stirring frequently, for 2–3 minutes, or until they give off their aroma. Remove from the pan and let cool.

2. Put the butter, superfine or granulated sugar, lemon zest, and toasted seeds into a large bowl and beat together until light and fluffy, then beat in the egg yolk. Sift the flour and salt into the mixture and stir until combined.

3. Halve the dough and shape it into two balls, then wrap in plastic wrap and chill in the refrigerator for 30–60 minutes.

4. Preheat the oven to 375°F. Line two large baking sheets with parchment paper.

5. Unwrap the dough and roll out between two sheets of parchment paper. Cut out circles with a 2½-inch plain, round cutter and place them on the prepared baking sheets, spaced well apart.

6. Bake in the preheated oven for 10–12 minutes, or until light golden brown. Let cool on the baking sheets for a few minutes, then transfer to wire racks to cool completely.

7. To make the glaze, sift the confectioners' sugar into a bowl, add the lemon extract, and gradually stir in the water to form a smooth icing with the consistency of thick cream. With the cooled cookies on the racks, spread the icing over them. Let set.

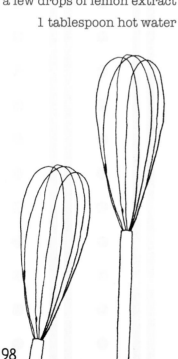

1

5

7

Chocolate & Almond Biscotti

makes 24

ingredients

unsalted butter, for greasing

1 cup blanched almonds

6 ounces semisweet chocolate, broken into pieces

2 cups all-purpose flour, plus extra for dusting

1 teaspoon baking powder

¾ cup superfine sugar or granulated sugar

2 extra-large eggs, lightly beaten

1 teaspoon vanilla extract

1. Preheat the oven to 325°F. Lightly grease a large baking sheet. Spread out the almonds on a separate baking sheet and bake in the preheated oven for 5–10 minutes, or until toasted. Let cool.

2. Put the chocolate into a heatproof bowl set over a saucepan of gently simmering water and stir until melted. Remove from the heat and let cool.

3. Sift the flour and baking powder into a large bowl. Add the sugar, toasted almonds, melted chocolate, eggs, and vanilla extract and mix together to form a soft dough.

4. Turn out the dough onto a lightly floured surface and, with floured hands, knead for 2–3 minutes, or until smooth. Divide the dough in half and shape each portion into a log shape about 2 inches in diameter. Place the logs on the prepared baking sheet and flatten until each is about 1 inch thick.

5. Bake in the preheated oven for 20–30 minutes, or until firm to the touch. Let cool on the baking sheet for 15 minutes. Meanwhile, reduce the oven temperature to 300°F.

6. Using a serrated knife, cut the baked dough into ½ inch-thick slices and place on ungreased baking sheets. Bake in the oven for 10 minutes. Turn and bake for an additional 10–15 minutes, until crisp. Transfer to wire racks to cool completely.

Maple & Pecan Cookies

makes 18

ingredients

¾ cup pecan halves

1 stick unsalted butter,
softened, plus extra
for greasing

2 tablespoons maple syrup

⅓ cup firmly packed light
brown sugar

1 extra-large egg yolk,
lightly beaten

1 cup all-purpose flour

1 teaspoon baking powder

1. Preheat the oven to 375°F. Lightly grease two baking sheets. Reserve 18 pecan halves and coarsely chop the rest.

2. Put the butter, maple syrup, and sugar into a bowl and beat together with a wooden spoon until light and fluffy. Beat in the egg yolk. Sift in the flour and baking powder, then add the chopped pecans. Mix to form a stiff dough.

3. Place 18 spoonfuls of the dough on the prepared baking sheets, spaced well apart. Top each with one of the reserved pecan halves, pressing down gently.

4. Bake in the preheated oven for 10–12 minutes, until light golden brown. Let cool on the baking sheets for a few minutes, then transfer to wire racks to cool completely.

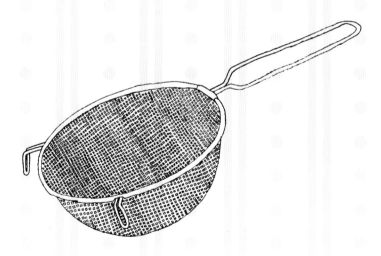

hints & tips

For an indulgent variation, drizzle melted chocolate over the cooled cookies.

Crisp & Crumbly
CHAPTER 3

Golden Hazelnut Cookies

makes 30

ingredients

2 sticks unsalted butter, softened

¾ cup superfine sugar or granulated sugar

1 egg yolk, lightly beaten

1¾ cups all-purpose flour

pinch of salt

½ cup ground hazelnuts

topping

8 ounces semisweet chocolate, broken into pieces

30 hazelnuts

1. Put the butter and sugar into a bowl and mix well with a wooden spoon, then beat in the egg yolk. Sift the flour and salt into the mixture, add the ground hazelnuts, and stir until thoroughly combined.

2. Halve the dough and shape into two balls, then wrap in plastic wrap and chill in the refrigerator for 30–60 minutes.

3. Preheat the oven to 375°F. Line two baking sheets with parchment paper.

4. Unwrap the dough and roll out between two sheets of parchment paper. Stamp out circles with a 2½-inch plain, round cutter and put them on the prepared baking sheets, spaced well apart.

5. Bake in the preheated oven for 10–12 minutes, until golden brown. Let cool on the baking sheets for a few minutes, then transfer to wire racks to cool completely.

6. When the cookies are cool, place the wire racks over a sheet of parchment paper. Put the chocolate into a heatproof bowl set over a saucepan of gently simmering water and stir until melted. Remove the bowl from the heat and let cool slightly, then spoon the chocolate over the cookies. Gently tap the wire racks to level the surface, add a hazelnut to the center of each cookie, and let set.

Crisp & Crumbly
CHAPTER 3

Orange & Lemon Cookies

makes 30

ingredients

2 sticks unsalted butter, softened

¾ cup superfine sugar or granulated sugar

1 egg yolk, lightly beaten

2¼ cups all-purpose flour

pinch of salt

finely grated zest of 1 orange

finely grated zest of 1 lemon

topping

1 tablespoon lightly beaten egg white

1 tablespoon lemon juice

1 cup confectioners' sugar

yellow food coloring

orange food coloring

15 lemon jelly candies

15 orange jelly candies

1. Put the butter and superfine or granulated sugar into a bowl and mix well with a wooden spoon, then beat in the egg yolk. Sift the flour and salt into the mixture and stir until thoroughly combined.

2. Halve the dough and gently knead the orange zest into one half and the lemon zest into the other. Shape into two balls, wrap in plastic wrap, and chill in the refrigerator for 30–60 minutes.

3. Preheat the oven to 375°F. Line two baking sheets with parchment paper.

4. Unwrap the orange-flavored dough and roll out between two sheets of parchment paper. Stamp out 15 circles with a 2½-inch plain, round cutter and put them on one of the prepared baking sheets, spaced well apart. Repeat with the lemon-flavored dough, but stamp out crescents.

5. Bake in the preheated oven for 10–15 minutes, until golden brown. Let cool on the baking sheets for a few minutes, then transfer to wire racks to cool completely.

6. Mix together the egg white and lemon juice. Gradually beat in the confectioners' sugar with a wooden spoon until smooth. Spoon half the glaze into a separate bowl. Stir yellow food coloring into one bowl and orange food coloring into the other. Leaving the cookies on the wire racks, spread the orange icing over the orange-flavored cookies and the yellow icing over the lemon-flavored cookies. Decorate with the jelly candies and let set.

hints & tips

To make crescents, stamp out circles, then cut away a section with the same cutter.

Iced Cherry Rings

makes 18

ingredients

1 stick unsalted butter, plus extra for greasing

⅓ cup superfine sugar or granulated sugar

1 egg yolk

finely grated zest of ½ lemon

1⅔ cups all-purpose flour, plus extra for dusting

¼ cup finely chopped candied cherries

lemon glaze

⅔ cup confectioners' sugar

1½ tablespoons lemon juice

1. Preheat the oven to 400°F. Lightly grease two large baking sheets.

2. Put the butter and superfine or granulated sugar into a large bowl and beat together until light and fluffy. Beat in the egg yolk and lemon zest. Sift in the flour and stir, then fold in the candied cherries and mix to form a soft dough.

3. Roll out the dough on a lightly floured surface to ¼ inch thick. Stamp out 3¼-inch circles with a plain, round cutter, then stamp out the center of each with a 1-inch plain, round cutter. Place the rings on the prepared baking sheets. Reroll any scraps and cut out more cookies.

4. Bake in the preheated oven for 12–15 minutes, or until golden. Let cool on the baking sheets for a few minutes, then transfer to wire racks to cool completely.

5. To make the glaze, mix the confectioners' sugar and lemon juice until smooth. Drizzle the icing over the cookies and let set.

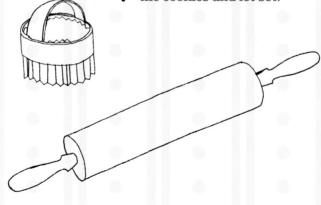

Granola Cookies

makes 24

ingredients

1 stick unsalted butter,
softened, plus extra
for greasing

⅓ cup raw brown sugar

1 tablespoon honey

1 cup all-purpose flour

1 teaspoon baking powder

pinch of salt

½ cup chopped dried apricots

¼ cup chopped dried figs

1¼ cups rolled oats

1 teaspoon milk, if needed

⅓ cup dried cranberries or
golden raisins

⅓ cup chopped walnuts

1. Preheat the oven to 325°F. Grease two large baking sheets.

2. Put the butter, sugar, and honey into a saucepan and heat over low heat until melted. Mix to combine. Sift the flour, baking powder, and salt into a large bowl and stir in the apricots, figs, and oats. Pour in the butter-and-sugar mixture and mix to form a dough. If it is too stiff, add a little milk.

3. Divide the dough into 24 pieces and roll each piece into a ball. Place the balls on the prepared baking sheets, spaced well apart, and press flat to a diameter of 2½ inches. Mix together the cranberries or golden raisins and walnuts and press into the cookies.

4. Bake in the preheated oven for 15 minutes. Let cool completely on the baking sheets.

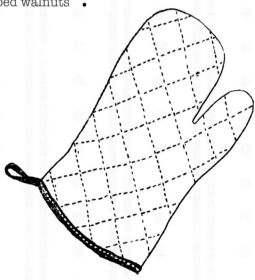

hints & tips

Use your favorite combo of dried fruits and nuts in this versatile recipe.

Crisp & Crumbly
CHAPTER 3

Carrot Cake Cookies

makes 30

ingredients

1 stick unsalted butter, softened

⅓ cup superfine sugar or granulated sugar

⅓ cup firmly packed light brown sugar

1 extra-large egg

½ teaspoon vanilla extract

1¼ cups all-purpose flour

½ teaspoon baking soda

½ teaspoon ground cinnamon

¾ cup grated carrots

¼ cup chopped walnuts

⅓ cup flaked dried coconut

1. Preheat the oven to 375°F. Line several large baking sheets with parchment paper.

2. Put the butter and sugars into a large bowl and beat together until pale and creamy. Beat the egg and vanilla extract into the mixture until smooth. Sift in the flour, baking soda, and cinnamon, then beat together until well combined. Add the grated carrots, chopped walnuts, and coconut to the mixture and mix together well.

3. Drop tablespoonfuls of the dough onto the prepared baking sheets, spaced well apart.

4. Bake in the preheated oven for 8–10 minutes, or until lightly golden brown around the edges. Let cool on the baking sheets for a few minutes, then transfer to wire racks to cool completely.

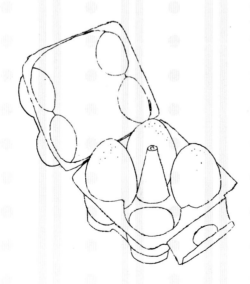

Margarita Cookies

makes 30

ingredients

2 sticks unsalted butter, softened

¾ cup superfine sugar or granulated sugar

finely grated zest of 1 lime

1 egg yolk, lightly beaten

1 teaspoon orange extract

2¼ cups all-purpose flour

pinch of salt

tequila glaze

1¼ cups confectioners' sugar

1–2 tablespoons white tequila

1. Preheat the oven to 375°F. Line two baking sheets with parchment paper.

2. Put the butter, superfine or granulated sugar, and lime zest into a bowl and mix well with a wooden spoon, then beat in the egg yolk and orange extract. Sift the flour and salt into the mixture and stir until thoroughly combined.

3. Scoop up tablespoonfuls of the dough and put them on the prepared baking sheets, spaced well apart, then flatten gently.

4. Bake in the preheated oven for 10–15 minutes, until light golden brown. Let cool on the baking sheets for a few minutes, then transfer to wire racks to cool completely.

5. Sift the confectioners' sugar into a bowl and stir in enough of the tequila to give the mixture the consistency of thick cream. Leaving the cookies on the wire racks, drizzle the icing over them with a teaspoon. Let set.

Almond Tuiles Dipped in Chocolate

makes 24

ingredients

1 teaspoon peanut oil

6 tablespoons unsalted butter, softened

⅓ cup superfine sugar or granulated sugar

⅓ cup all-purpose flour

pinch of salt

¾ cup slivered almonds

6 ounces semisweet chocolate, broken into pieces

1. Preheat the oven to 400°F. Brush two large baking sheets with the oil.

2. Put the butter and sugar into a large bowl and beat together until light and fluffy. Sift in the flour and salt and fold into the mixture, then add the slivered almonds and mix together.

3. Drop tablespoonfuls of the dough onto the prepared baking sheets, spaced well apart, and spread into flat ovals with the back of a spoon.

4. Bake, one baking sheet at a time, in the preheated oven for 5 minutes, or until golden. While the cookies are still warm, lift each one in turn and drape over a wooden rolling pin to make a curved shape. Let harden for 1 minute, then transfer to a wire rack to cool completely.

5. Place the chocolate in a heatproof bowl set over a saucepan of gently simmering water and stir until melted. Remove from the heat and let cool slightly. Dip one end of each of the tuiles into the melted chocolate, transfer to a sheet of parchment paper or a wire rack, and let set.

CHAPTER 4
FUN & DECORATIVE

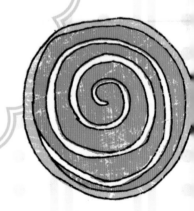

Button Cookies

makes 26

ingredients

1¾ sticks unsalted butter, softened

¾ cup superfine sugar or granulated sugar

1 extra-large egg

2 teaspoons vanilla extract

3¼ cups all-purpose flour

food coloring pastes in 3 different colors of your choice

1. Line two baking sheets with parchment paper.

2. In a large bowl, cream the butter and sugar with an electric mixer until just coming together. Add the egg and vanilla extract and briefly beat together.

3. Add the flour and use a wooden spoon to mix everything together to make a coarse dough. Gather into a ball with your hands, then divide into three equal portions. Knead a different food coloring into each portion of dough. Wrap each portion of dough in plastic wrap and chill in the refrigerator for at least 10 minutes.

4. Unwrap the dough and roll out each portion between two large sheets of parchment paper, turning the dough occasionally until it is an even thickness of about ¼ inch. Using a 3¼-inch plain, round cutter, stamp out about 26 cookies in total, rerolling each dough as necessary.

5. Transfer the cookies to the prepared baking sheets. Lightly press a 2-inch plain, round cutter into the center of each cookie to make an indentation (don't cut all the way through), then use the tip of a plain piping tip to make four button holes in the center of each. Chill in the refrigerator for 10 minutes. Meanwhile, preheat the oven to 350°F.

6. Bake the cookies in the preheated oven for 15–18 minutes, or until just turning golden at the edges. Let cool on the baking sheets for a few minutes, then transfer to wire racks to cool completely.

Fun & Decorative
CHAPTER 4

Stacked Heart Cookies

makes 14

ingredients

1⅔ cups all-purpose flour,
plus extra for dusting

1 stick unsalted butter, diced

½ cup superfine sugar or
granulated sugar

1 egg, lightly beaten

½ teaspoon vanilla extract

royal icing

1 extra-large egg white,
lightly beaten

1¾ cups confectioners' sugar,
sifted

a few drops of warm water,
if needed

pink food coloring paste

1. Sift the flour into a large bowl. Add the diced butter and rub into the flour until the mixture resembles fine bread crumbs. Stir in the sugar followed by the egg and vanilla extract and mix to form a crumbly dough.

2. Gather together the dough with your hands and gently knead on a lightly floured surface until smooth. Wrap the dough in plastic wrap and chill in the refrigerator for 1 hour. Line two large baking sheets with parchment paper.

3. Unwrap the dough and roll out on a lightly floured surface to a thickness of ¼ inch. Using 2¾-inch and 1¼-inch heart-shape cutters, stamp out 14 large and 14 small cookies, rerolling the dough as necessary. Place on the prepared baking sheets and chill in the refrigerator for an additional 20 minutes. Preheat the oven to 350°F.

4. Bake in the preheated oven for 10–12 minutes, or until pale golden around the edges. Let cool on the baking sheets for a few minutes, then transfer to wire racks to cool completely.

5. To make the icing, put the egg white into a large bowl. Gradually beat in the confectioners' sugar to make a smooth, thick icing. Add a few drops of warm water, if needed, to create the correct consistency. Reserve 1 tablespoon of the icing in a small bowl and cover the surface with plastic wrap to prevent it from drying out.

6. Spoon one-third of the remaining icing into a separate bowl and color it pink. Spoon into a pastry bag fitted with a fine plain tip and pipe a thin outline around each cookie. Let set for 10 minutes.

7. Gently spoon a little of the white icing into the center of one of the large cookies and ease to the piped outline with a teaspoon. Shake the cookie gently to flatten the icing and remove any air bubbles with the tip of a toothpick. Repeat to fill all the large cookies.

8. Pipe pink dots onto the white icing. Pipe the remaining pink icing into the small cookie hearts, easing the icing to the outline with a toothpick. Let the iced cookies stand on a wire rack to set for 3–4 hours, or overnight. Spread the bottom of the small cookies with a little of the reserved white icing, then gently place on top of the large cookies. Let set.

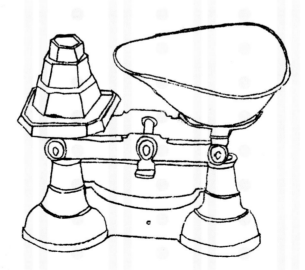

3

6

8

hints & tips

You can make these cookies in
whatever shapes you desire. Stacked
star cookies would make the perfect
Christmas gift.

Fun & Decorative
CHAPTER 4

Handprint Cookies

makes 20

ingredients

1¾ sticks unsalted butter, softened

¾ cup superfine sugar or granulated sugar

1 extra-large egg

2 teaspoons vanilla extract

3¼ cups all-purpose flour

to decorate

1 egg white, lightly beaten or 2 tablespoons cooled, boiled water

edible glitter sugar in a color of your choice

1. Line two baking sheets with parchment paper.

2. In a large bowl, cream the butter and sugar with an electric mixer until just coming together. Add the egg and vanilla extract and briefly beat together.

3. Add the flour and use a wooden spoon to mix everything together to form a coarse dough. Gather the dough into a ball with your hands, wrap in plastic wrap, and chill in the refrigerator for at least 10 minutes.

4. Unwrap the dough and roll out between two large sheets of parchment paper, turning the dough occasionally until it is an even thickness of about ¼ inch. Stamp out 20 handprint shapes, using a shaped cutter or by cutting around a template, rerolling the dough as necessary.

5. Transfer the cookies to the prepared baking sheets and chill in the refrigerator for 10 minutes. Meanwhile, preheat the oven to 350°F.

6. Bake in the preheated oven for 15–18 minutes, or until just turning golden at the edges. Let cool on the baking sheets for a few minutes, then transfer to wire racks to cool completely.

7. To decorate, use a small paintbrush to brush a little of the egg white over the fingertips of the cookies and sprinkle with glitter sugar. Hold a small shaped cutter in place over each palm, brush a little more of the egg white inside the shape, then sprinkle with the glitter sugar.

4

6

7

Quilted Cookies

makes 18

ingredients

4 tablespoons unsalted butter, softened, plus extra for greasing

⅓ cup superfine sugar or granulated sugar

1 teaspoon finely grated orange zest

1 egg, lightly beaten

1⅓ cups all-purpose flour

to decorate

3 tablespoons confectioners' sugar, sifted

½ teaspoon warm water

10 ounces white ready-to-use fondant

pink and blue food coloring pastes

edible silver balls

1. Place the butter, superfine or granulated sugar, and orange zest in a large bowl and beat together until pale and creamy. Beat in the egg, then sift in the flour and mix to form a crumbly dough. Gather together with your hands and knead lightly on a floured surface until smooth. Wrap in plastic wrap and chill in the refrigerator for 30 minutes. Lightly grease two baking sheets.

2. Unwrap the dough and roll out between two large sheets of parchment paper to a thickness of about ¼ inch. Using a 2¾-inch fluted square cutter, stamp out 18 cookies, rerolling the dough as necessary. Place on the prepared baking sheets, spaced well apart. Chill in the refrigerator for 20 minutes. Preheat the oven to 375°F.

3. Bake in the preheated oven for 10–12 minutes, or until set and pale golden around the edges. Let cool on the baking sheets for a few minutes, then transfer to wire racks to cool completely.

4. Mix together the confectioners' sugar and water to form a spreadable icing and set aside.

5. Color half of the fondant pink and half blue by kneading in a little of each food coloring paste. Roll out the pink fondant between two sheets of parchment paper to a thickness of ⅛ inch and, using the same square cutter, stamp out nine squares. Spread a little of the icing onto half the cookies and top with the pink squares. Repeat with the blue fondant and remaining cookies.

6. Use a thin knife to gently score a diamonds across the top of each cookie. Decorate with silver balls to create a quilted effect, pressing them into the icing. Let stand in a cool place until the fondant is firm.

2

5

5

Fun & Decorative
CHAPTER 4

Lollipop Swirl Cookies

makes 12

ingredients

1¾ sticks unsalted butter,
softened

¾ cup superfine sugar or
granulated sugar

1 extra-large egg

2 teaspoons vanilla extract

3¼ cups all-purpose flour

12 lollipop sticks

royal icing

3⅔ cups confectioners'
sugar, sifted

2 tablespoons plus 1 teaspoon
egg white powder

⅓ cup water

food coloring pastes in
3 different colors
of your choice

1. Line three baking sheets with parchment paper.

2. In a large bowl, cream the butter and superfine or granulated sugar with an electric mixer until just coming together. Add the egg and vanilla extract and briefly beat together.

3. Add the flour and use a wooden spoon to mix everything together to form a coarse dough. Gather into a ball with your hands, wrap in plastic wrap, and chill in the refrigerator for at least 10 minutes.

4. Unwrap the dough and roll out between two large sheets of parchment paper, turning the dough occasionally until it is an even thickness of about ½ inch. Stamp out about 12 circles using a 3¼-inch plain, round cutter, rerolling the dough as necessary.

5. Transfer the cookies to the prepared baking sheets, leaving room for the lollipop sticks. Dip one end of a lollipop stick in water and then carefully insert it into the center of the bottom of a cookie, pushing it in about halfway into the cookie. Repeat with the remaining lollipop sticks and cookies. Chill in the refrigerator for 10 minutes. Meanwhile, preheat the oven to 350°F.

6. Bake in the preheated oven for 15–18 minutes, or until just turning golden at the edges. Let cool on the baking sheets for a few minutes, then transfer to wire racks to cool completely.

7. To make the royal icing, sift the confectioners' sugar into a large mixing bowl, then add the egg white powder and water. Stir with a spoon until the icing is smooth and combined. Next, use an electric mixer to beat the mixture for 3–4 minutes, or until it becomes thick and is the texture of toothpaste.

8. Spoon one-quarter of the icing into a pastry bag fitted with a fine plain tip. Cover the remaining icing with damp paper towels. Carefully pipe a border around the edge of each cookie and let set for 10 minutes. Meanwhile, preheat the oven to 120–160°F or the lowest setting.

9. To make the runny or "flood" icing, add water to the remaining icing, a drop at a time, beating between additions, until the icing is the consistency of Greek-style yogurt. Divide the icing evenly among four bowls and add a different food coloring to three of the bowls. Spoon each of the icings into a squeezy bottle or a pastry bag fitted with a plain tip.

10. One at a time, invert a squeezy bottle of colored icing and direct the runny icing inside the piped border of a cookie to "flood" and fill inside the border with the icing. Next, take the squeezy bottle of white icing and, starting in the center, pipe a spiral onto each cookie (on top of the colored icings). Gently tap the cookies to make any air bubbles rise to the surface and pop them with a toothpick.

11. Return the cookies to the preheated oven to dry for about 40 minutes; they are ready when the icing is nice and hard. Transfer the cookies to a wire rack and let cool completely.

5

hints & tips
You need only a tiny amount of food coloring paste to create an intense color. To avoid adding too much, dip a toothpick into the food coloring and stir into the icing.

10

10

133

Message Cookies

makes 30

ingredients

2 sticks unsalted butter, softened

¾ cup superfine sugar or granulated sugar

1 egg yolk, lightly beaten

2 teaspoons orange juice or orange liqueur

finely grated zest of 1 orange

2¼ cups all-purpose flour

pinch of salt

royal icing

1 egg white

1¾ cups confectioners' sugar

food coloring paste in the color of your choice

1. Put the butter and sugar into a large bowl and beat together until light and fluffy, then beat in the egg yolk, orange juice, and orange zest. Sift the flour and salt into the mixture and stir until combined. Halve the dough and shape into two balls, then wrap in plastic wrap and chill in the refrigerator for 30–60 minutes.

2. Preheat the oven to 375°F. Line two large baking sheets with parchment paper.

3. Unwrap the dough and roll out to a thickness of about ⅛ inch. Depending on the occasion, stamp out appropriate shapes with cookie cutters and transfer to the prepared baking sheets, spaced well apart.

4. Bake in the preheated oven for 10–15 minutes, or until light golden brown. Let cool on the baking sheets for a few minutes, then transfer to wire racks to cool completely.

5. Put the egg white and confectioners' sugar into a bowl and beat until smooth, adding a little water, if necessary. Transfer two-thirds of the icing to a separate bowl, then stir in a few drops of food coloring paste. Put the white icing in a pastry bag fitted with a fine tip.

6. Spread the colored icing over the top of the cookies, using the back of a spoon. Pipe dots of the white icing around the edges of each cookie, on top of the colored icing, and add the message of your choice. Let set.

Piñata Cookies

makes 10

ingredients

1¾ sticks unsalted butter, softened

¾ cup superfine sugar or granulated sugar

1 extra-large egg

2 teaspoons vanilla extract

3 cups all-purpose flour

¼ cup unsweetened cocoa powder

4 ounces white chocolate, broken into pieces

6 ounces small candy-coated chocolates or other small candies of your choice

sprinkles, to decorate

1. Line two baking sheets with parchment paper.

2. Put the butter and sugar into a bowl and beat with an electric mixer until light and fluffy, then beat in the egg and vanilla extract. Divide the creamed mixture evenly between two bowls. Sift 1⅔ cups of the flour into one bowl and mix together to form a coarse dough. Gather into a ball with your hands, wrap in plastic wrap, and chill in the refrigerator for at least 10 minutes. Sift the remaining flour and the cocoa into the other bowl and mix together to make a coarse dough. Gather, wrap, and chill the dough as before.

3. Place one ball of dough between two sheets of parchment paper and roll out to a thickness of about ¼ inch. Repeat with the second ball of dough. Stamp out 25 cookies from each dough using a 2½-inch plain, round cutter, rerolling the dough as necessary.

4. Transfer ten vanilla and ten cocoa cookies to the prepared baking sheets. Using a 1½-inch plain, round cutter, remove a circle from the center of the remaining cookies. Transfer to the prepared baking sheets and chill in the refrigerator for 10 minutes. Meanwhile, preheat the oven to 350°F.

5. Bake in the preheated oven for 15–18 minutes, or until the vanilla cookies are golden. Let cool on the baking sheets for a few minutes, then transfer to wire racks to cool completely.

6. To assemble, put the white chocolate in a small heatproof bowl set over a saucepan of gently simmering water and stir until melted. Remove from the heat and let cool for 10 minutes.

7. Spoon the cooled melted chocolate into a paper pastry bag and use scissors to snip off the tip. Take a solid vanilla cookie and pipe a circle of melted chocolate around the edge, then top with a cocoa ring. Repeat this process to attach a vanilla ring and then another cocoa ring (making a total of four layers). Fill the hollow in the center of the rings with the candies.

8. Finally, pipe melted chocolate around the edge of the uppermost cocoa ring and top with another solid vanilla cookie. Repeat to make nine more stacks the same way, but starting with a cocoa solid cookie for five of the stacks and alternating the colors as before.

9. Pipe any remaining melted chocolate in zigzags over the top of the stacks, then decorate with sprinkles. Let set.

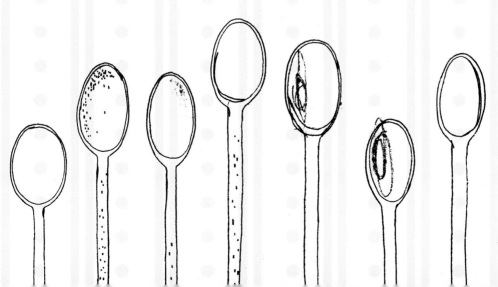

2

4

7

hints & tips

Instead of the melted chocolate, you could use a simple icing made from confectioners' sugar and water to stick the cookie layers together.

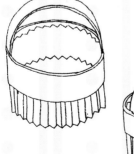

Matchstick Cookies

makes 30

ingredients

5 tablespoons unsalted butter,
softened, plus extra for greasing

¼ cup superfine sugar or
granulated sugar

1 teaspoon grated lemon zest

1 egg yolk

1 cup all-purpose flour,
plus extra for dusting

1 tablespoon cornstarch

royal icing

1 tablespoon egg white,
lightly beaten

⅔ cup confectioners'
sugar, sifted

a few drops of lemon juice

pink food coloring paste

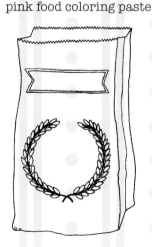

1. Put the butter, superfine or granulated sugar, and lemon zest in a large bowl and beat together until pale and creamy. Beat in the egg yolk, then sift in the flour and cornstarch and mix to form a coarse dough. Gather together with your hands and knead lightly on a floured surface until smooth. Roll into a log shape, then wrap in plastic wrap and chill in the refrigerator for 45 minutes. Lightly grease two baking sheets.

2. Roll out the dough on a lightly floured surface to a thickness of about ¼ inch. Cut into 30 thin sticks each measuring ¼ inch wide by 3½ inches long, rerolling the dough as necessary. Place on the prepared baking sheets and chill in the refrigerator for an additional 20 minutes. Preheat the oven to 375°F.

3. Bake in the preheated oven for 7–9 minutes, or until pale golden. Let cool on the baking sheets for a few minutes, then transfer to wire racks to cool completely.

4. To make the icing, place the egg white in a bowl and gradually beat in the confectioners' sugar and lemon juice to make a thick icing. Beat in a little pink food coloring to create a pale pink color.

5. Gently dip one end of each matchstick cookie in the icing. Place on a wire rack with the iced ends hanging over the edge of the rack and let set.

hints & tips

For added sparkle, dip the iced ends of the cookies in pink edible glitter sugar.

Fun & Decorative
CHAPTER 4

Double Heart Cookies

makes 30

ingredients

1 envelope instant latte

1½ teaspoons hot water

2 sticks unsalted butter, softened

¾ cup superfine sugar or granulated sugar

1 egg yolk, lightly beaten

2 cups all-purpose flour

2 pinches of salt

1 teaspoon vanilla extract

3 tablespoons unsweetened cocoa powder

1. Put the instant latte into a small bowl and stir in the hot water to make a paste. Put the butter and sugar into a separate bowl and mix well with a wooden spoon, then beat in the egg yolk. Divide the mixture between two bowls. Beat the latte paste into one bowl. Sift in 1¼ cups of the flour and a pinch of salt into the mixture and stir. Shape the dough into a ball, wrap in plastic wrap, and chill in the refrigerator for 30–60 minutes.

2. Beat the vanilla extract into the other bowl, then sift in the remaining flour, the cocoa, and a pinch of salt and stir. Shape the dough into a ball, wrap in plastic wrap, and chill as before.

3. Preheat the oven to 375°F. Line two baking sheets with parchment paper.

4. Unwrap both dough balls and roll out each one between two sheets of parchment paper. Stamp out 15 cookies from each layer of dough with a 2¾-inch heart-shape cutter and put them on the prepared baking sheets, spaced well apart. Using a 1½–2-inch heart-shape cutter, stamp out the centers of each larger heart and remove from sheets. Put a small cocoa-flavored heart in the center of each large coffee-flavored heart and vice versa.

5. Bake in the preheated oven for 10–15 minutes. Let cool on the baking sheets for a few minutes, then transfer to wire racks to cool completely.

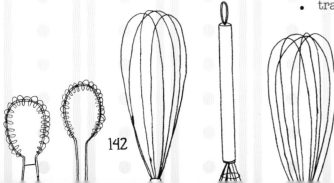

142

hints & tips
For triple heart cookies,
use three different sizes of
cookie cutters.

Fun & Decorative
CHAPTER 4

Moustache Cookie Pops

makes 24

ingredients

1¾ sticks unsalted butter, softened

¾ cup superfine sugar or granulated sugar

1 extra-large egg

2 teaspoons vanilla extract

3¼ cups all-purpose flour

24 lollipop sticks

edible writing pens or writing icing, to decorate

royal icing

3⅔ cups confectioners' sugar, sifted

2 tablespoons plus 1 teaspoon egg white powder

⅓ cup water

1. Line two or three baking sheets with parchment paper.

2. In a large bowl, cream the butter and superfine or granulated sugar with an electric mixer until just coming together. Add the egg and vanilla extract and briefly beat together. Add the flour and use a wooden spoon to mix everything together to make a coarse dough. Gather into a ball with your hands, wrap in plastic wrap, and chill in the refrigerator for at least 10 minutes.

3. Meanwhile, draw various moustache shapes on stiff cardboard with a pencil, then cut out to make moustache-shape templates.

4. Roll out the dough between two large sheets of parchment paper, turning the dough occasionally, until it is a thickness of about ¼ inch. Use a knife to cut around the templates to make 24 moustache shapes, rerolling the dough as necessary.

5. Transfer the cookies to the prepared baking sheets, leaving room for the lollipop sticks. Dip the end of a lollipop stick in water and then carefully insert it into the bottom of a cookie. Repeat with the remaining lollipop sticks and cookies. Chill in the refrigerator for 10 minutes. Meanwhile, preheat the oven to 350°F.

6. Bake in the preheated oven for 15–18 minutes, or until just turning golden at the edges. Let cool on the baking sheets for a few minutes, then transfer to wire racks to cool completely.

7. To make the royal icing, sift the confectioners' sugar into a large mixing bowl, then add the egg white powder and water. Stir with a spoon until the icing is smooth and combined. Next, use an electric mixer to beat the mixture for 3–4 minutes, or until it becomes thick and is the texture of toothpaste.

8. Spoon one-quarter of the icing into a pastry bag fitted with a fine plain tip. Cover the remaining icing with damp paper towels. Carefully pipe a border around the edge of each cookie and let set for 10 minutes. Meanwhile, preheat the oven to 120–160°F or the lowest setting.

9. To make the runny or "flood" icing, add water to the remaining icing, a drop at a time, beating between additions, until the icing is the consistency of Greek-style yogurt.

10. Fill a squeezy bottle or pastry bag fitted with a plain tip with the runny icing. Invert the squeezy bottle and direct the runny icing inside the piped border of a cookie to "flood" and fill inside the border with the icing. Gently tap the cookie to make any air bubbles rise to the surface and pop them with a toothpick. Repeat with the rest of the cookies and runny icing.

11. Return the cookies to the preheated oven for about 40 minutes; they are ready when the icing is nice and hard. Transfer the cookies to wire racks and let cool completely.

12. To finish, use edible writing pens or writing icing to decorate each moustache cookie and make it look wonderfully hairy. Let dry before serving.

4

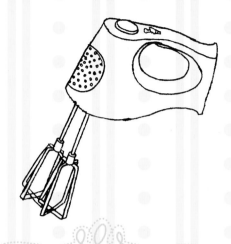

hints & tips

Instead of using the writing pens to decorate the cookies, sprinkle chocolate sprinkles over the icing while it is wet for really hairy looking moustaches.

7

10

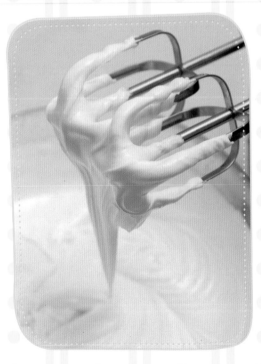

147

Tutti Frutti Whoopie Pies

makes 25

ingredients

2 cups all-purpose flour

1 teaspoon baking soda

large pinch of salt

1 stick unsalted butter, softened

¾ cup superfine sugar or granulated sugar

1 extra-large egg, beaten

½ teaspoon vanilla extract

⅔ cup buttermilk

½ cup finely chopped, mixed colored candied cherries

¼ cup sprinkles

marshmallow filling

32 white marshmallows (about 8 ounces)

¼ cup milk

a few drops of pink food coloring paste

½ cup vegetable shortening

⅓ cup confectioners' sugar, sifted

1. Preheat the oven to 350°F. Line two or three large baking sheets with parchment paper. Sift the flour, baking soda, and salt into a large bowl and set aside.

2. Put the butter and superfine or granulated sugar into a large bowl and beat with an electric mixer until pale and fluffy. Beat in the egg and vanilla extract followed by half the flour mixture and then the buttermilk. Stir in the rest of the flour mixture and mix until thoroughly incorporated. Stir in the candied cherries.

3. Pipe or spoon 50 small mounds of the dough onto the prepared baking sheets, spaced well apart.

4. Bake in the preheated oven for 9–11 minutes, until risen and just firm to the touch. Let cool on the baking sheets for a few minutes, then transfer to wire racks to cool completely.

5. For the filling, place the marshmallows, milk, and food coloring in a heatproof bowl set over a saucepan of gently simmering water. Heat until the marshmallows have melted, stirring occasionally. Remove from the heat and let cool.

6. Put the vegetable shortening and confectioners' sugar into a bowl and beat together until smooth and creamy. Add the creamed mixture to the cooled marshmallow mixture and beat for 1–2 minutes, until fluffy.

7. To assemble, spread the filling over the flat side of half of the whoopie pies. Top with the remaining whoopie pies. Spread the sprinkles on a plate and gently roll the edges of each whoopie pie in them to lightly coat.

hints & tips

These cute and colorful mini whoopie pies are perfect for parties.

Fun & Decorative
CHAPTER 4

149

Multicolor
Iced Spiced Cookies

makes 16

ingredients

1 stick unsalted butter,
softened, plus extra
for greasing

¼ cup superfine sugar or
granulated sugar

1 egg, lightly beaten

1¾ cups all-purpose flour,
plus extra for dusting

½ teaspoon baking powder

2 teaspoons ground allspice

royal icing

1 extra-large egg white,
lightly beaten

1¾ cups confectioners'
sugar, sifted

a few drops of warm water,
if needed

yellow and blue food
coloring pastes

1. Put the butter and superfine or granulated sugar into a large bowl and beat together until pale and creamy. Gradually beat in the egg, then sift in the flour, baking powder, and allspice and mix to form a crumbly dough. Gather together with your hands and knead lightly on a floured surface until smooth. Wrap in plastic wrap and chill in the refrigerator for 30 minutes. Preheat the oven to 350°F. Lightly grease two large baking sheets.

2. Roll out the dough on a lightly floured surface to a thickness of ¼ inch. Using a 2¾-inch plain, round cutter, stamp out 16 circles, rerolling the dough as necessary. Transfer to the prepared baking sheets. Bake in the preheated oven for 10–12 minutes, or until pale golden. Let cool on the baking sheets for a few minutes, then transfer to wire racks to cool completely.

3. To make the icing, put the egg white into a large bowl. Gradually beat in the confectioners' sugar to make a smooth, thick icing. Add a few drops of warm water, if needed, to get the correct consistency. Spoon two tablespoons of the icing into a small bowl and color it yellow. Spoon another two tablespoons of icing into a second small bowl and color it blue. Spoon the colored icings into separate small paper pastry bags and snip off the ends.

4. Working with one cookie at a time, spread a little of the white icing over the top, right up to the edges. While the icing is still wet, pipe parallel lines of colored icing across the white icing. Drag the tip of a toothpick across the lines. Alternatively, pipe concentric circles of colored icing on top of the white icing, then drag the tip of a toothpick through the icing from the center to the edge and back again. Let set.

Fun & Decorative
CHAPTER 4

Gingerbread Men

makes 16

ingredients

3⅔ cups all-purpose flour,
plus extra for dusting

2 teaspoons ground ginger

1 teaspoon baking soda

1 stick unsalted butter,
plus extra for greasing

⅓ cup light corn syrup

¾ cup firmly packed light
brown sugar

1 extra-large egg, beaten

48 small candy-coated
chocolates, to decorate

royal icing

1 tablespoon egg white,
lightly beaten

⅔ cup confectioners'
sugar, sifted

a few drops of lemon juice

1. Preheat the oven to 350°F. Lightly grease two large baking sheets. Sift the flour, ginger, and baking soda into a large bowl and set aside.

2. Put the butter, light corn syrup, and brown sugar into a saucepan and gently heat until syrupy. Add the flour mixture together with the egg and mix to form a firm dough.

3. Roll out the dough on a lightly floured work surface to a thickness of ½ inch. Using a shaped cutter, stamp out 16 gingerbread men, rerolling the dough as necessary. Place on the prepared baking sheets, spaced well apart.

4. Bake in the preheated oven for 10–15 minutes, until golden brown. Let cool on the baking sheets for a few minutes, then transfer to wire racks to cool completely.

5. To make the icing, put the egg white into a bowl and gradually beat in the confectioners' sugar and lemon juice to make a thick icing.

6. Spoon the icing into a pastry bag fitted with a fine plain tip and use to decorate the gingerbread men with faces and bow ties. Attach the chocolate candies for buttons with a little of the icing. Let set.

2

3

6

CHAPTER 5

SOMETHING SPECIAL

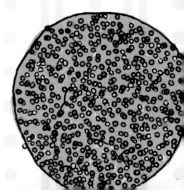

Crunchy Nut & Honey Cookie Sandwiches

makes 30

ingredients

2½ sticks unsalted butter, softened

¾ cup superfine sugar or granulated sugar

1 egg yolk, lightly beaten

2 teaspoons vanilla extract

2¼ cups all-purpose flour

pinch of salt

⅓ cup coarsely chopped pine nuts

⅔ cup confectioners' sugar

⅓ cup thick honey

1. Preheat the oven to 375°F. Line two baking sheets with parchment paper.

2. Put 2 sticks of the butter and the superfine or granulated sugar into a bowl and mix well with a wooden spoon, then beat in the egg yolk and vanilla extract. Sift the flour and salt into the mixture and stir until thoroughly combined.

3. Scoop up tablespoons of the dough and roll into balls. Put half of them on one of the prepared baking sheets, spaced well apart, and flatten gently. Spread out the pine nuts in a shallow dish and dip one side of the remaining dough balls into them, then place on the other baking sheet, nut side uppermost, and flatten gently.

4. Bake in the preheated oven for 10–15 minutes, until light golden brown. Let cool on the baking sheets for a few minutes, then transfer to wire racks to cool completely.

5. Beat the remaining butter with the confectioners' sugar and honey until creamy and thoroughly mixed. Spread the honey mixture over the plain cookies and top with the nut-coated cookies.

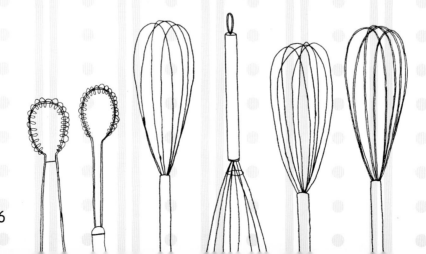

hints & tips

Try using pecans and maple syrup instead of the pine nuts and honey.

Alphabet Cookies

makes 24

ingredients

1¾ sticks unsalted butter, softened

¾ cups superfine sugar or granulated sugar

1 extra-large egg

2 teaspoons vanilla extract

3¼ cups all-purpose flour

buttercream

⅔ cup confectioners' sugar

¼ cup unsweetened cocoa powder

4 tablespoons unsalted butter, softened

1–2 tablespoons milk

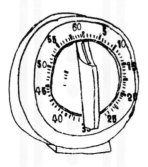

1. In a large bowl, cream the butter and superfine or granulated sugar with an electric mixer until just coming together. Add the egg and vanilla extract and briefly beat. Add the flour and use a wooden spoon to mix together to form a coarse dough. Gather into a ball with your hands, wrap in plastic wrap, and chill in the refrigerator for at least 10 minutes. Line two large baking sheets with parchment paper.

2. Unwrap the dough and roll out between two large sheets of parchment paper, turning the dough occasionally until it is a thickness of about ¼ inch. Using a 2½-inch plain, round cutter, stamp out 48 circles, rerolling the dough as necessary.

3. Transfer the cookies to the prepared baking sheets. Next, stamp out letter shapes from half of the cookies (so you end up with 24 round shapes and 24 letter shapes). Chill in the refrigerator for 10 minutes. Meanwhile, preheat the oven to 350°F.

4. Bake in the preheated oven for 15–18 minutes, or until just turning golden at the edges. Let cool on the baking sheets for a few minutes, then transfer to wire racks to cool completely.

5. To make the buttercream, sift the confectioners' sugar and cocoa into a large bowl, then add the butter and milk. Using an electric mixer, beat the ingredients together until combined, smooth and fluffy.

6. Sandwich the cookies together with the buttercream, spreading it on the bottom of the plain cookies and then topping each with a letter cookie. Let set before serving.

3

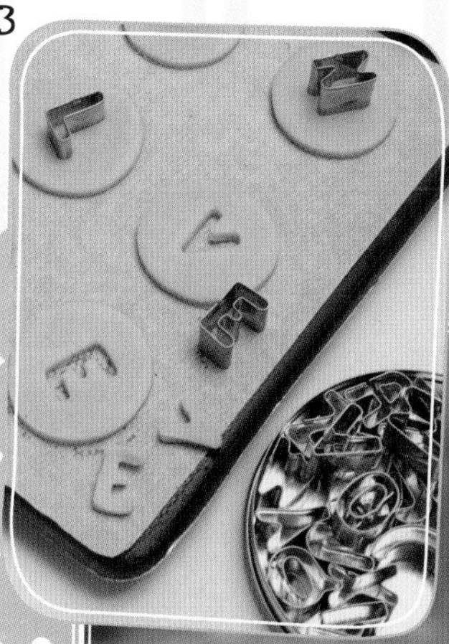

5

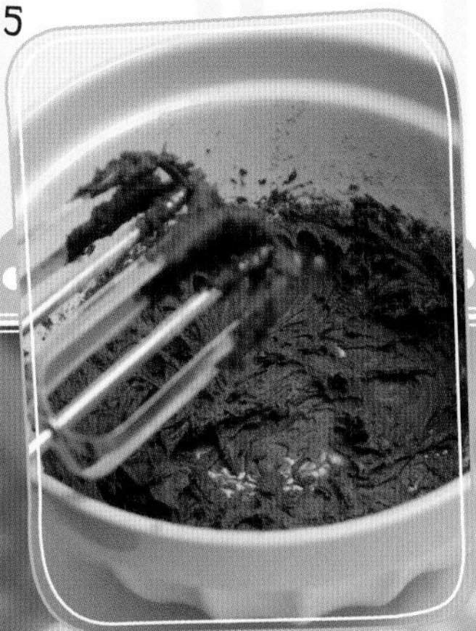

6

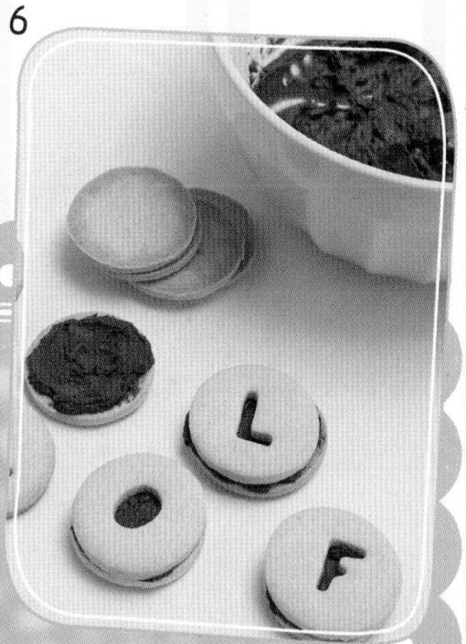

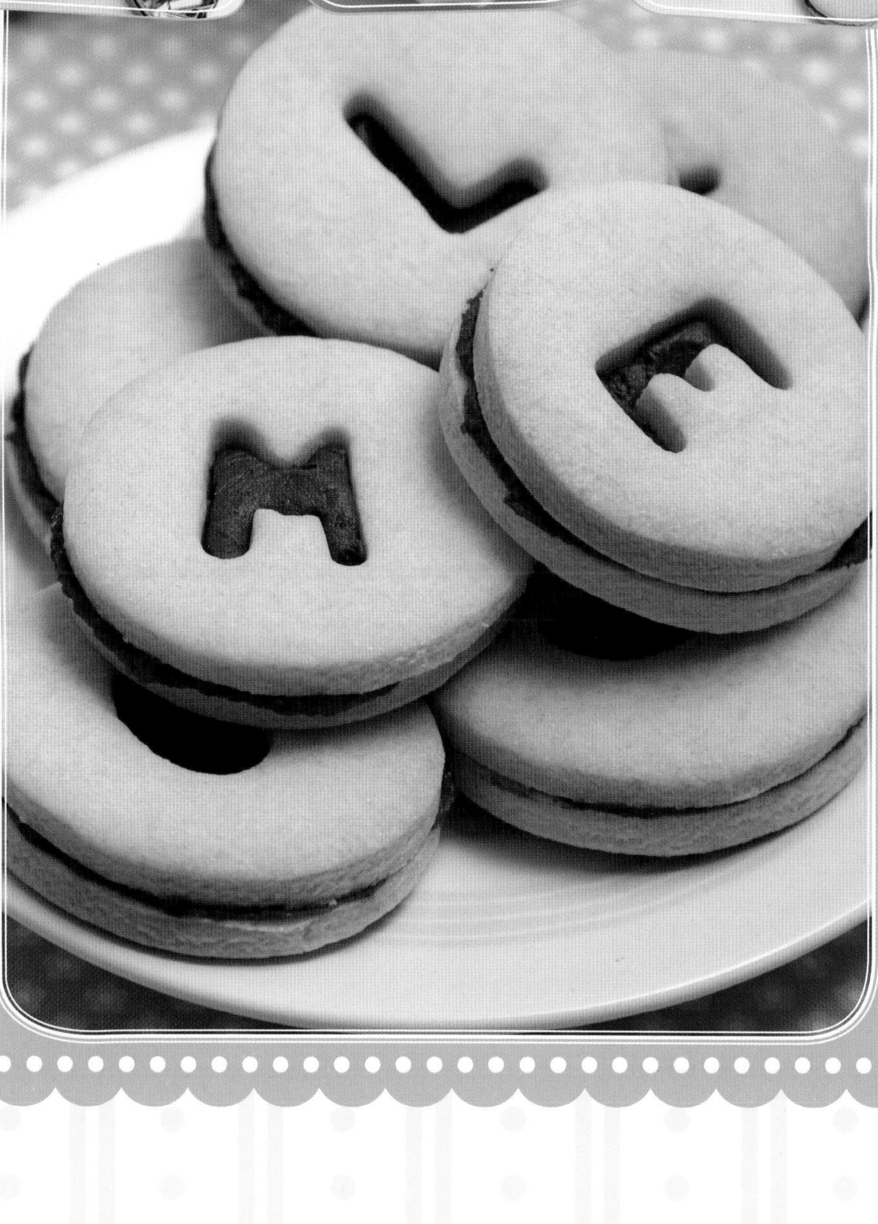

Rainbow Swirl Cookies

makes 28

ingredients

2 sticks unsalted butter, softened, plus extra for greasing

¾ cup superfine sugar or granulated sugar

1 egg yolk

1 teaspoon vanilla extract

2¼ cups all-purpose flour, plus extra for dusting

yellow, red, and blue food coloring pastes

1 tablespoon lightly beaten egg white

1. Put the butter and sugar into a large bowl and beat together until pale and creamy. Beat in the egg yolk and vanilla extract, then sift in the flour and mix to form a soft dough. Knead lightly on a floured surface until smooth.

2. Divide the dough into three equal pieces. Knead some yellow food coloring into one third, adding extra flour to prevent the dough from getting too sticky. Color the other two pieces of dough red and blue in the same way. Shape each colored dough into a 6 inch-long log and wrap in plastic wrap. Chill in the refrigerator for 1 hour.

3. Unwrap the dough and roll out each piece on a floured surface to form an 8 x 10-inch rectangle. Carefully lift and place the rectangles of dough on top of each other. Lightly brush the top with egg white, then roll up tightly from one long side like a jellyroll. Wrap in plastic wrap and chill for 40–50 minutes, or until firm.

4. Preheat the oven to 350°F. Grease two large baking sheets.

5. Unwrap the dough and cut into 28 slices, each about ½ inch thick. Place on the prepared baking sheets, spaced well apart.

6. Bake in the preheated oven for 10–12 minutes, or until just firm. Let cool on the baking sheets for a few minutes, then transfer to wire racks to cool completely.

2

3

5

Stained-Glass Window Cookies

makes 25

ingredients

2¾ cups all-purpose flour,
plus extra for dusting

pinch of salt

1 teaspoon baking soda

1 stick unsalted butter

¾ cup superfine sugar or
granulated sugar

1 extra-large egg

1 teaspoon vanilla extract

¼ cup light corn syrup

50 boiled fruit-flavor candies
(about 9 ounces)

1. Sift the flour, salt, and baking soda into a large bowl, add the butter, and rub it in until the mixture resembles bread crumbs. Stir in the sugar. Put the egg, vanilla extract, and light corn syrup into a separate bowl and whisk together. Pour into the flour mixture and mix to form a smooth dough. Shape the dough into a ball, wrap in plastic wrap, and chill in the refrigerator for 30 minutes.

2. Preheat the oven to 350°F. Line two large baking sheets with parchment paper.

3. Unwrap the boiled candies, separate into the different colors, and coarsely chop. Set aside.

4. Unwrap the dough and roll out on a lightly floured work surface to a thickness of ¼ inch. Using a 2¾-inch plain, round cutter, stamp out 25 circles, rerolling the dough as necessary.

5. Transfer the cookies to the prepared baking sheets and stamp out shapes from the centers of the cookies. Fill the holes with the chopped candy.

6. Bake in the preheated oven for 10–12 minutes, or until the candies are melted. Let cool on the baking sheets until the centers have hardened.

1

3

5

Cookies & Cream Sandwiches

makes 15

ingredients

1 stick unsalted butter, softened

⅔ cup confectioners' sugar

1 cup all-purpose flour

½ cup unsweetened cocoa powder

½ teaspoon ground cinnamon

filling

4 ounces semisweet chocolate, broken into pieces

¼ cup heavy cream

1. Preheat the oven to 325°F. Line two large baking sheets with parchment paper.

2. Put the butter and confectioners' sugar into a large bowl and beat together until light and fluffy. Sift the flour, cocoa, and cinnamon into the mixture and mix to form a dough.

3. Place the dough between two sheets of parchment paper and roll out to a thickness of ⅛ inch. Stamp out 30 circles using a 2½-inch plain, round cutter, rerolling the dough as necessary. Transfer to the prepared baking sheets.

4. Bake in the preheated oven for 15 minutes, or until firm to the touch. Let cool on the baking sheets for a few minutes, then transfer to wire racks to cool completely.

5. Meanwhile, make the filling. Put the chocolate and cream into a saucepan and heat gently until the chocolate has melted. Stir until smooth. Let cool, then chill in the refrigerator for 2 hours, or until firm. Sandwich the cookies together in pairs with a spoonful of the filling.

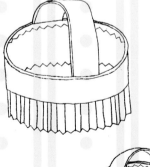

3

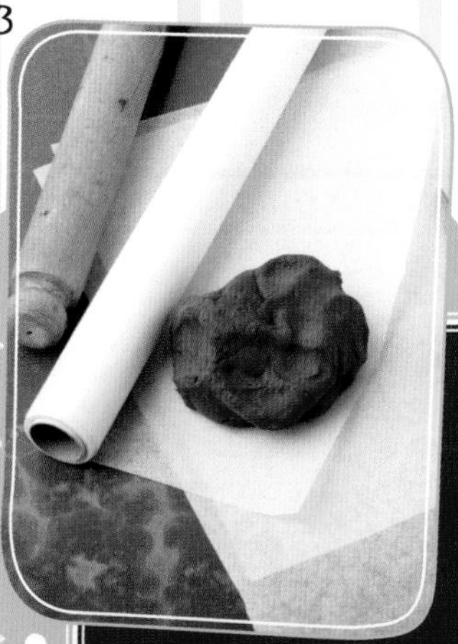

3

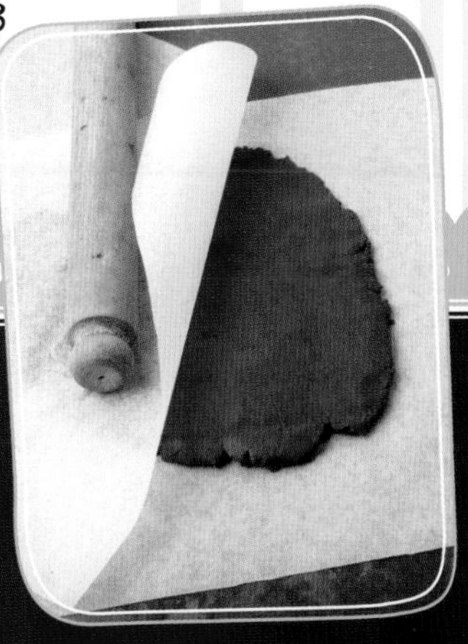

3

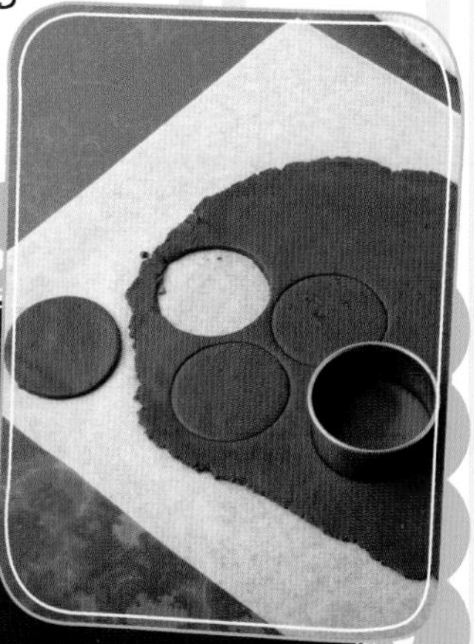

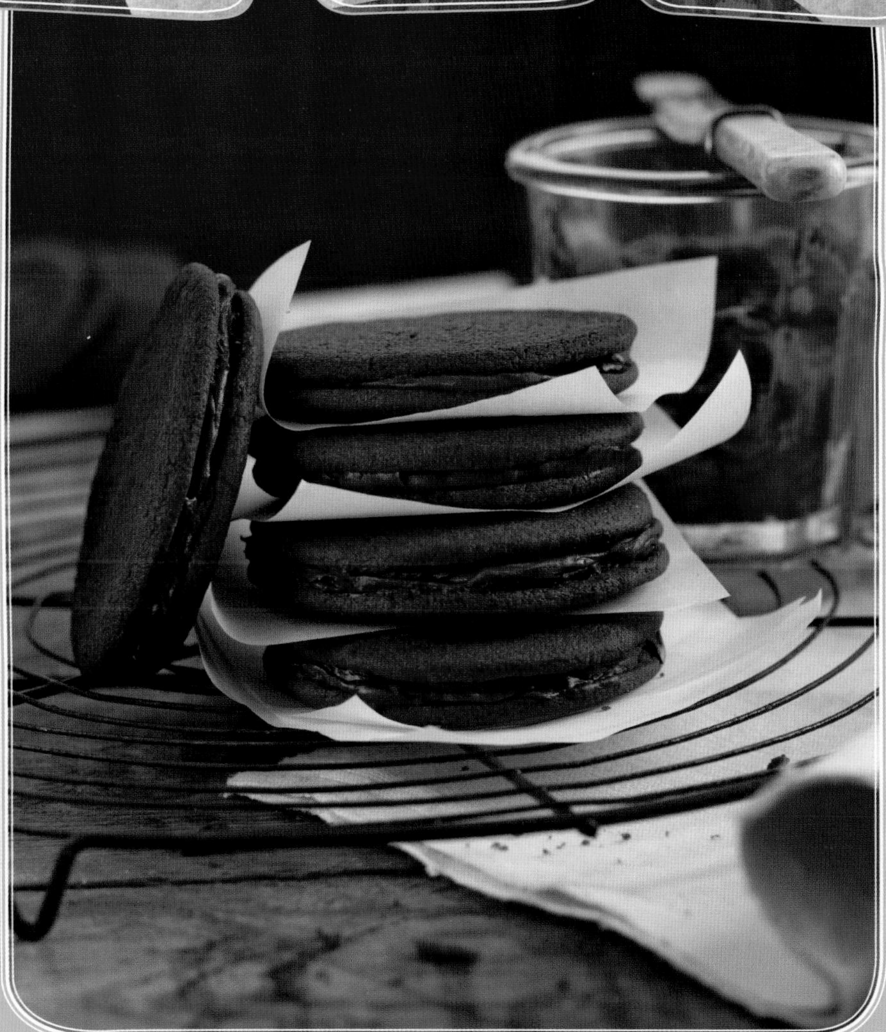

Apple Spice Cookies

makes 15

ingredients

2 sticks unsalted butter, softened

¾ cup superfine sugar or granulated sugar

1 egg yolk, lightly beaten

2 teaspoons apple juice

2¼ cups all-purpose flour

½ teaspoon ground cinnamon

½ teaspoon apple pie spice

pinch of salt

1 cup finely chopped dried apple

filling

1 tablespoon superfine sugar or granulated sugar

1 tablespoon custard powder or instant vanilla pudding and pie filling mix

½ cup milk

⅓ cup applesauce

1. Put the butter and sugar into a large bowl and beat together until light and fluffy, then beat in the egg yolk and apple juice. Sift the flour, cinnamon, apple pie spice, and salt into the mixture. Add the apple and stir until combined. Halve the dough and shape into two balls, then wrap in plastic wrap and chill in the refrigerator for 30–60 minutes.

2. Preheat the oven to 375°F. Line two large baking sheets with parchment paper.

3. Unwrap the dough and roll out between two sheets of parchment paper. Stamp out 30 cookies using a 2-inch fluted square cutter and place them on the prepared baking sheets, spaced well apart.

4. Bake in the preheated oven for 10–15 minutes, or until light golden brown. Let cool on the baking sheets for a few minutes, then transfer to wire racks to cool completely.

5. To make the filling, mix together the sugar, custard powder or vanilla pudding and pie filling mix, and milk in a saucepan. Bring to a boil, stirring constantly, and cook until thickened. Remove from the heat and stir in the applesauce. Cover the surface with plastic wrap and let cool.

6. Sandwich the cookies together in pairs with a spoonful of the cooled filling.

hints & tips

Omit the filling and dip the cookies in melted white chocolate instead.

Mint Cookies with White Chocolate Ganache

makes 15

ingredients

2 sticks unsalted butter, softened

¾ cup superfine sugar or granulated sugar

1 egg yolk, lightly beaten

2 teaspoons vanilla extract

2¼ cups all-purpose flour

pinch of salt

4 ounces chocolate mint sticks or candy bars, finely chopped

confectioners' sugar, for dusting

white chocolate filling

2 tablespoons heavy cream

4 ounces white chocolate, broken into pieces

1. Put the butter and superfine or granulated sugar into a large bowl and beat together until light and fluffy, then beat in the egg yolk and vanilla extract. Sift the flour and salt into the mixture, add the chocolate sticks, and stir until combined. Halve the dough and shape into two balls, then wrap in plastic wrap and chill in the refrigerator for 30–60 minutes.

2. Preheat the oven to 375°F. Line two large baking sheets with parchment paper.

3. Unwrap the dough and roll out between two sheets of parchment paper. Stamp out 30 cookies with a 2½-inch fluted, round cutter and place them on the prepared baking sheets, spaced well apart.

4. Bake in the preheated oven for 10–15 minutes, or until light golden brown. Let cool on the baking sheets for a few minutes, then transfer to wire racks to cool completely.

5. To make the filling, pour the cream into a saucepan, add the chocolate, and melt over low heat, stirring occasionally, until smooth. Let cool, then chill in the refrigerator until the mixture has a spreadable consistency.

6. Spread the filling over half the cookies and top with the remaining cookies, then dust with confectioners' sugar.

hints & tips

Replace the white chocolate in the ganache with semisweet mint chocolate.

Something Special
CHAPTER 5

Marshmallow Cookie Sandwiches

makes 20

ingredients

marshmallow

sunflower oil, for greasing

1 tablespoon cornstarch

1 tablespoon confectioners' sugar

1 cup cold water

2½ cups granulated sugar

½ cup hot water

3½ tablespoons powdered gelatin

2 extra-large egg whites

1 teaspoon vanilla extract

cookies

1 stick unsalted butter, softened, plus extra for greasing

¼ cup superfine sugar or granulated sugar

1 egg yolk

1⅓ cups all-purpose flour, plus extra for dusting

8 ounces semisweet chocolate, broken into pieces

1. Lightly oil a 9 x 13-inch jellyroll pan. Line the bottom and two short sides with parchment paper, then lightly oil the paper.

2. Sift the cornstarch and confectioners' sugar into a bowl. Use a little of this mixture to dust the lined pan, tapping it firmly so the mixture coats the bottom and sides completely.

3. Put the cold water and granulated sugar into a small, deep saucepan. Heat gently, stirring constantly with a wooden spoon, until the sugar has dissolved. Bring the syrup to a boil and boil, without stirring, for about 5 minutes, until the mixture reaches around 248°F on a candy thermometer (the firm ball stage).

4. Meanwhile, put the hot water into a small bowl, sprinkle the gelatin over it, and stir until dissolved and the liquid is clear. Put the egg whites into the bowl of a freestanding electric mixer and beat until they hold stiff peaks.

5. When the syrup has reached the correct temperature, remove from the heat and add the gelatin mixture; it will fizz and bubble. Let stand for a few seconds, then slowly pour the syrup into a large, heatproof bowl (be careful, because the mixture will be extremely hot).

6. Turn the mixer on at low speed and gradually add the hot syrup in a slow, thin stream, beating constantly. When all the syrup has been added, increase the speed to high and beat for 10 minutes, until the mixture is thick and glossy and leaves a thick trail on the surface when the beaters are lifted. Beat in the vanilla extract.

7. Pour the batter into the prepared pan and gently level the surface. Lightly dust the top with a little of the cornstarch mixture. Let set, uncovered, in a cool dry place for 3–4 hours.

8. Meanwhile, make the cookies. Put the butter and superfine or granulated sugar into a bowl and beat with an electric mixer until pale and creamy. Beat in the egg yolk, then sift in the flour and mix to form a soft dough. Knead lightly until smooth, then wrap in plastic wrap and chill in the refrigerator for 45 minutes. Grease two large baking sheets.

9. Unwrap the dough and roll out thinly on a lightly floured surface. Use a 2½-inch cloud-shape cutter to stamp out 40 cookies, rerolling the dough as necessary. Place on the prepared baking sheets and chill in the refrigerator for 30 minutes. Preheat the oven 350°F.

10. Bake in the preheated oven for 10–12 minutes, or until pale golden. Let cool on the baking sheets for a few minutes, then transfer to wire racks to cool completely.

11. Put the chocolate into a heatproof bowl set over a saucepan of gently simmering water and stir until melted. Remove from the heat and let cool for 10 minutes. Dip one side of each cookie in the cooled melted chocolate, then place on a wire rack set over a baking sheet. Chill in the refrigerator until set.

12. To assemble the sandwich cookies, run the tip of a lightly greased knife along the unlined sides of the pan to release the marshmallow. Using the lining paper, gently lift out the marshmallow sheet and slide onto a cutting board.

13. Wipe clean and lightly grease the cloud cutter and use to stamp out 20 cloud shapes, washing, drying, and regreasing the cutter frequently. Toss all the cloud shapes in the remaining cornstarch mixture. Sandwich each marshmallow between two of the chocolate-coated cookies.

10

11

13

hints & tips

When adding the hot syrup and gelatin mixture to the beaten egg whites, make sure it hits the egg whites and not the beaters on the mixer or the sides of the bowl, where it will set instantly.

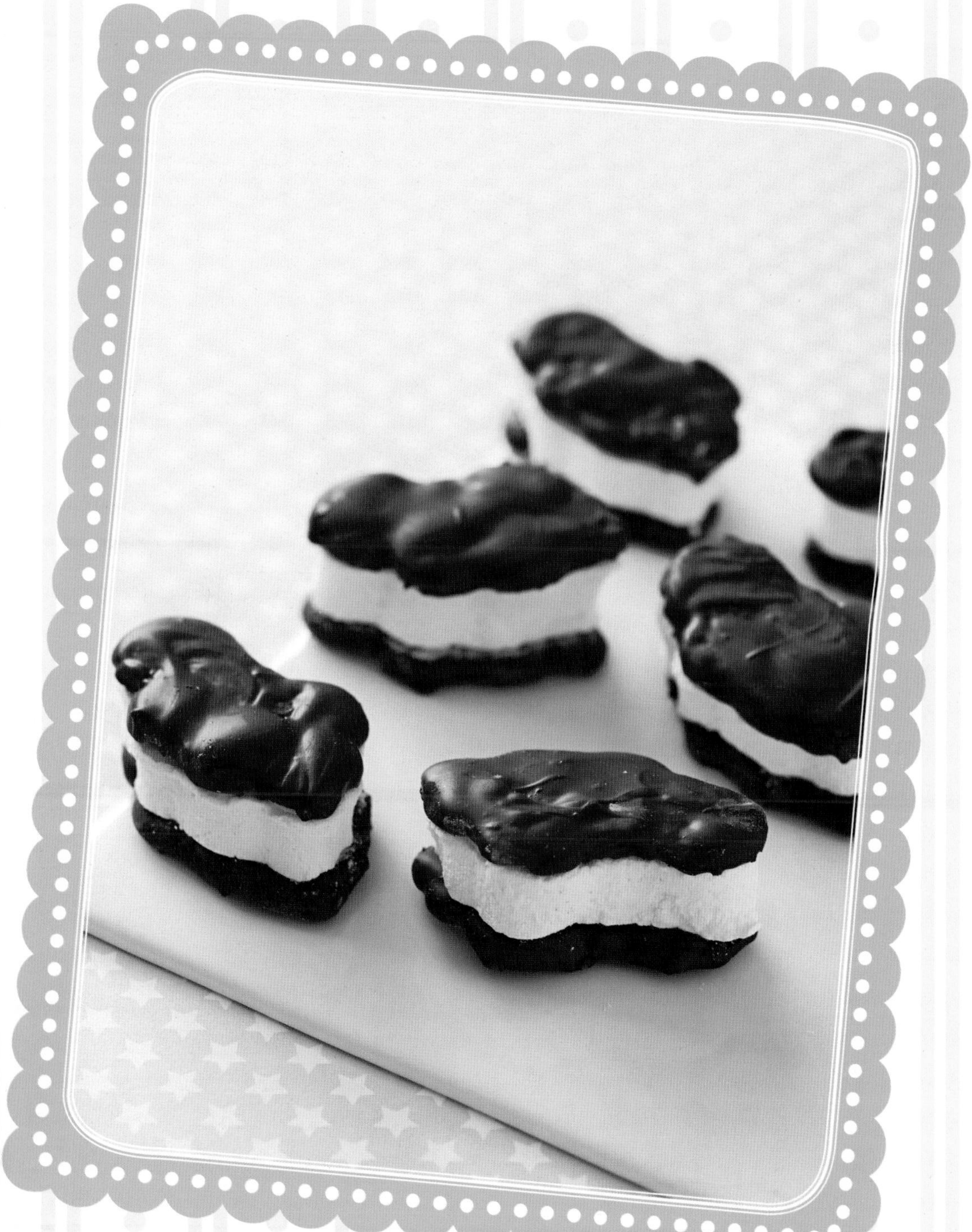

Ice Cream Cookie Sandwiches

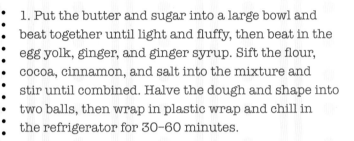

makes 30

ingredients

2 sticks unsalted butter, softened

¾ cup superfine sugar or granulated sugar

1 egg yolk, lightly beaten

2 tablespoons finely chopped preserved ginger, plus 2 teaspoons syrup from the jar

2 cups all-purpose flour

¼ cup unsweetened cocoa powder

½ teaspoon ground cinnamon

pinch of salt

2 cups ice cream

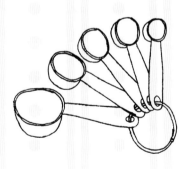

1. Put the butter and sugar into a large bowl and beat together until light and fluffy, then beat in the egg yolk, ginger, and ginger syrup. Sift the flour, cocoa, cinnamon, and salt into the mixture and stir until combined. Halve the dough and shape into two balls, then wrap in plastic wrap and chill in the refrigerator for 30–60 minutes.

2. Preheat the oven to 375°F. Line two large baking sheets with parchment paper.

3. Unwrap the dough and roll out between two sheets of parchment paper. Using a 2½-inch fluted, round cutter, stamp out 60 cookies and place them on the prepared baking sheets, spaced well apart.

4. Bake in the preheated oven for 10–15 minutes, or until light golden brown. Let cool on the baking sheets for a few minutes, then transfer to wire racks to cool completely.

5. Remove the ice cream from the freezer about 15 minutes before serving to let it soften. Put a generous scoop of ice cream on half the cookies and top with the remaining cookies. Press together gently so that the filling spreads to the edges. If not serving immediately, wrap the cookies individually in aluminum foil and store in the freezer.

Something Special
CHAPTER 5

Jelly Sandwich Cookies

makes 18

ingredients

1⅓ cups all-purpose flour,
plus extra for dusting

1 stick unsalted butter, diced,
plus extra for greasing

½ cup superfine sugar or
granulated sugar

1 egg, lightly beaten

½ teaspoon vanilla extract

filling

5 tablespoons unsalted butter,
softened

½ teaspoon vanilla extract

1¼ cups confectioners'
sugar, sifted

2 tablespoons strawberry jelly

1. Sift the flour into a large bowl. Add the diced butter and rub it into the flour with your fingertips until the mixture resembles fine bread crumbs. Stir in the superfine or granulated sugar, followed by the egg and vanilla extract and mix to form a crumbly dough. Gather together with your hands and knead lightly until smooth.

2. Roll the dough into a 7 inch-long log and wrap in plastic wrap. Shape the log into a square by smoothing with your hands and tapping firmly on a work surface. Use your finger and thumb to pinch the sides of the log to resemble a loaf of bread. Chill in the refrigerator for 1 hour 30 minutes, or until the dough is firm (reshape the dough after 30 minutes).

3. Preheat the oven to 350°F. Grease two large baking sheets.

4. Unwrap the dough and, using a thin knife, slice it into 36 slices, each about ¼ inch thick. Transfer to the prepared baking sheets.

5. Bake in the preheated oven for 10–12 minutes, or until pale golden around the edges. Let cool on the baking sheets for a few minutes, then transfer to wire racks to cool completely.

6. For the filling, put the butter and vanilla extract into a bowl and gradually beat in the confectioners' sugar until smooth and creamy. Sandwich together the cookies in pairs with the buttercream and jelly.

4   5   6

Something Special
CHAPTER 5

Chocolate & Ginger Checkerboard Cookies

makes 30

ingredients

2 sticks unsalted butter, softened

¾ cup superfine sugar or granulated sugar

1 egg yolk, lightly beaten

2 teaspoons vanilla extract

2¼ cups all-purpose flour

pinch of salt

1 teaspoon ground ginger

1 tablespoon finely grated orange zest

1 tablespoon unsweetened cocoa powder

1 egg white, lightly beaten

1. Put the butter and sugar into a bowl and mix well with a wooden spoon, then beat in the egg yolk and vanilla extract. Sift the flour and salt into the mixture and stir until thoroughly combined.

2. Divide the dough in half. Add the ginger and orange zest to one half and mix well. Shape the dough into a 6 inch-long log. Flatten the sides and top to square off the log and make it 2 inches high. Wrap in plastic wrap and chill in the refrigerator for 30-60 minutes. Add the cocoa to the other half of the dough and mix well. Shape into a flattened log as before, wrap in plastic wrap, and chill in the refrigerator for 30-60 minutes.

3. Unwrap the dough and cut each log lengthwise into three slices. Cut each slice lengthwise into three strips. Brush the strips with egg white and stack them in threes, alternating the flavors, to make two checkered log shapes. Wrap in plastic wrap and chill for 30-60 minutes.

4. Preheat the oven to 375°F. Line two baking sheets with parchment paper.

5. Unwrap the logs and cut into slices with a sharp, serrated knife. Transfer the cookies to the prepared baking sheets, spaced well apart.

6. Bake in the preheated oven for 12-15 minutes, until firm. Let cool on the baking sheets for a few minutes, then transfer to wire racks to cool completely.

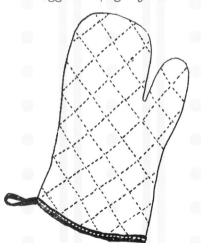

hints & tips

Create colorful effects by adding food coloring to the dough instead of cooca.

Rainbow Slice Cookies

makes 20

ingredients

1¾ sticks unsalted butter, softened

¾ cup superfine sugar or granulated sugar

1 extra-large egg

1 teaspoon vanilla extract

3¼ cups all-purpose flour

red, orange, yellow, green, blue, and purple food coloring pastes

to decorate

4 ounces white chocolate, broken into pieces

sprinkles

1. Line two baking sheets with parchment paper.

2. In a large bowl, cream the butter and sugar with an electric mixer until just coming together. Add the egg and vanilla extract and briefly beat together. Add the flour and use a wooden spoon to mix everything together to form a coarse dough.

3. Gather the dough into a ball with your hands, then divide it into six equal portions. Knead a different food coloring into each portion of dough, kneading each one separately on a clean surface so the colors don't merge. Wrap each portion of colored dough separately in plastic wrap and chill in the refrigerator for at least 10 minutes.

4. Unwrap the dough and roll out each portion between two large sheets of parchment paper, turning the dough occasionally until it is an even thickness of about ½ inch and forms a rectangle, about 8 x 4 inches. Stack up all the rolled-out rectangles of colored dough, one on top of another, then trim the edges so that you have a neat stack.

5. Slice the stack in half widthwise to make two 4 x 4-inch squares. Cut each square vertically into ten slices, with each cookie being just under ½ inch thick.

6. Transfer the cookies to the prepared baking sheets. Chill in the refrigerator for 10 minutes. Meanwhile, preheat the oven to 350°F.

7. Bake in the preheated oven for 15–18 minutes, or until just turning golden at the edges. Let the cookies rest on the baking sheets to cool completely.

8. To decorate, put the chocolate in a small heatproof bowl set over a saucepan of gently simmering water and stir until melted and smooth. Remove from the heat and let cool slightly. Dip one end of each cookie into the melted chocolate and place back on the parchment paper, then sprinkle with sprinkles and let set.

4

hints & tips

These bright colors can be easily achieved with natural food colorings, available online and from specialty kitchen stores.

8

5

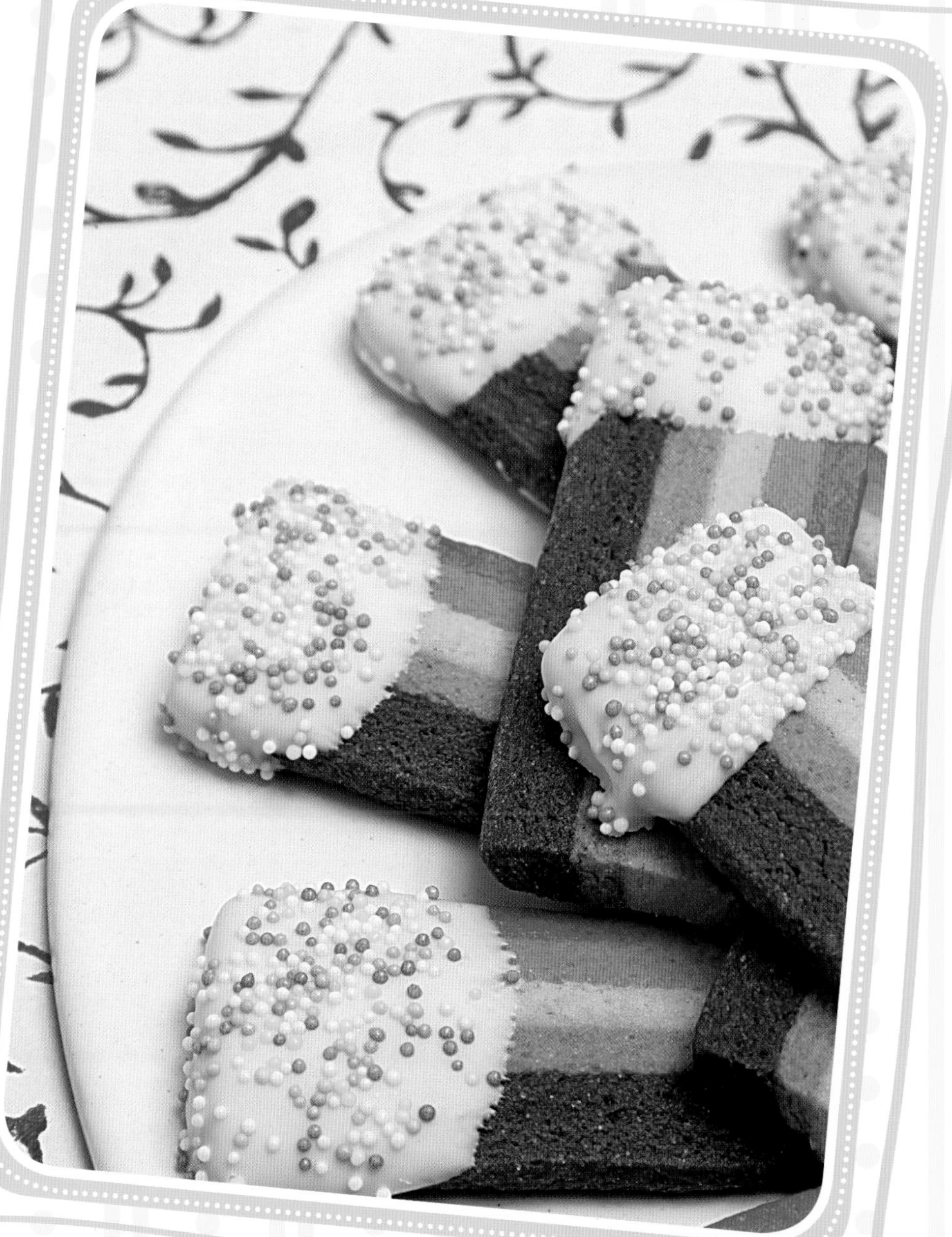

Red Velvet Cookies

makes 20

ingredients

1 stick unsalted butter, softened

1 cup superfine sugar or granulated sugar

1 extra-large egg, beaten

1 teaspoon vanilla extract

½ teaspoon white wine vinegar

1½ teaspoons red liquid food coloring

1¾ cups all-purpose flour

2 tablespoons unsweetened cocoa powder

¾ teaspoon baking powder

pinch of salt

3 ounces white chocolate, broken into pieces

1. Preheat the oven to 375°F. Line two large baking sheets with parchment paper.

2. Put the butter and sugar into a large bowl and beat together until pale and creamy. Gradually beat in the egg, followed by the vanilla extract, vinegar, and food coloring. Sift in the flour, cocoa, baking powder, and salt. Stir until thoroughly blended to form a soft dough.

3. Shape the dough into 20 balls, each about the size of a golf ball. Place on the prepared baking sheets, spaced well apart, and flatten each one with your fingers.

4. Bake in the preheated oven for 10–12 minutes, or until just risen and set. Let cool on the baking sheets for a few minutes, then transfer to wire racks to cool completely.

5. Put the chocolate into a heatproof bowl set over a saucepan of gently simmering water and stir until melted and smooth. Spoon into a paper pastry bag and snip off the end. Pipe zigzag lines of chocolate over each cookie. Let set.

2

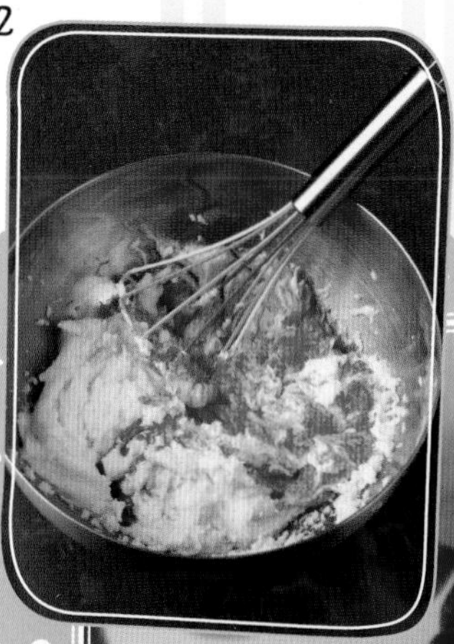

3

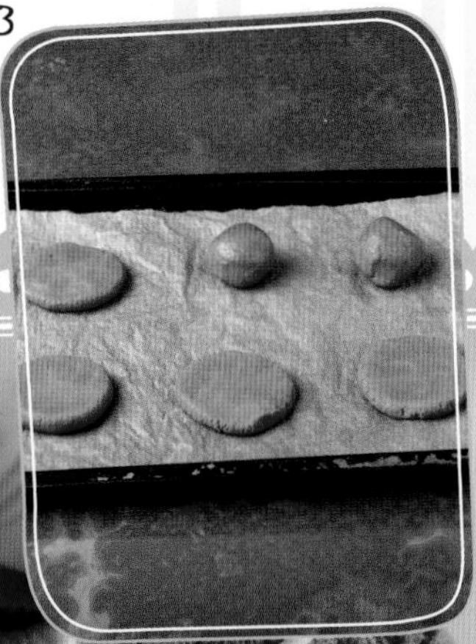

5

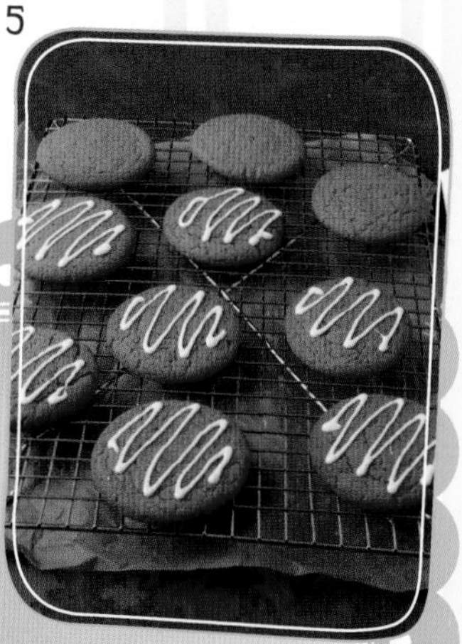

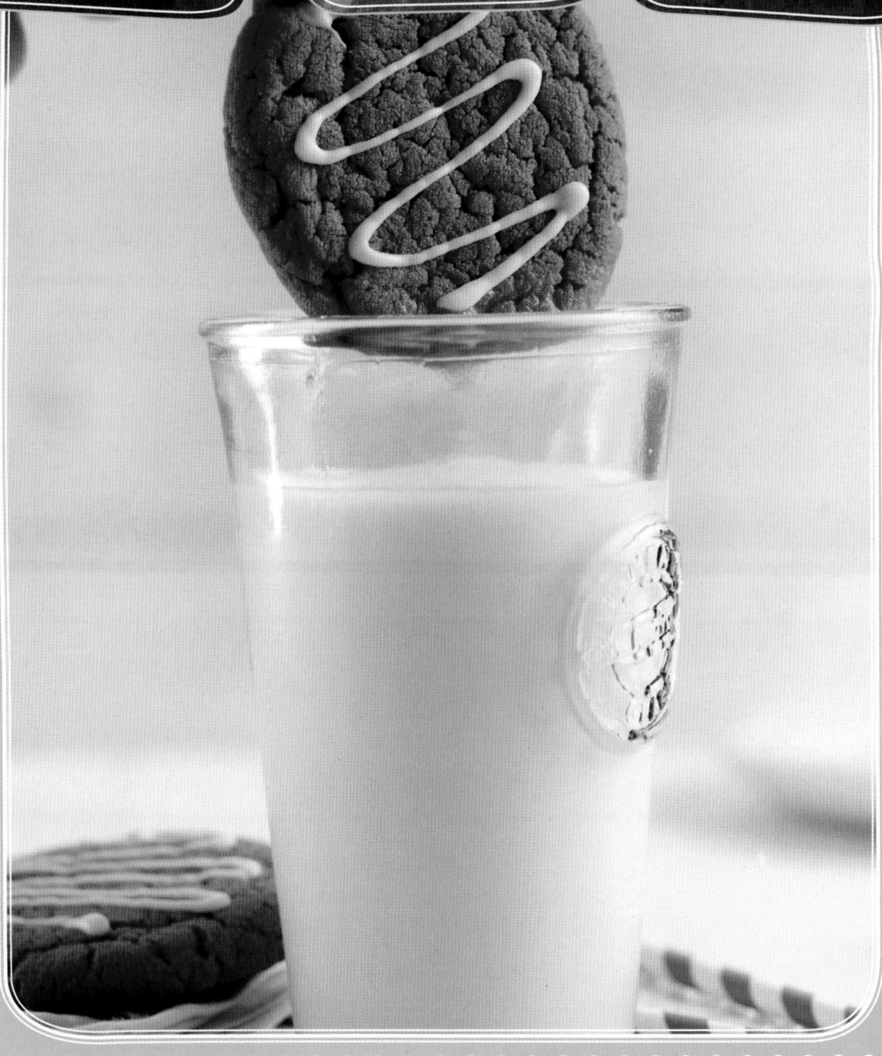

Rainbow Sprinkle Sugar Cookies

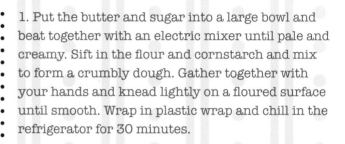

makes 18

ingredients

1 stick unsalted butter, softened, plus extra for greasing

⅓ cup superfine sugar or granulated sugar

¾ cup all-purpose flour, plus extra for dusting

⅓ cup cornstarch

1–2 tablespoons milk

¼ cup sprinkles

1. Put the butter and sugar into a large bowl and beat together with an electric mixer until pale and creamy. Sift in the flour and cornstarch and mix to form a crumbly dough. Gather together with your hands and knead lightly on a floured surface until smooth. Wrap in plastic wrap and chill in the refrigerator for 30 minutes.

2. Preheat the oven to 350°F. Grease two large baking sheets.

3. Unwrap the dough and roll out between two large sheets of parchment paper to a thickness of ¼ inch. Using a 2½-inch fluted, round cutter, stamp out 18 cookies, rerolling the dough as necessary.

4. Transfer the cookies to the prepared baking sheets. Brush the tops lightly with the milk and sprinkle liberally with the sprinkles, pressing down gently with your fingertips.

5. Bake in the preheated oven for 10–12 minutes, or until pale golden. Let cool on the baking sheets for a few minutes, then transfer to wire racks to cool completely.

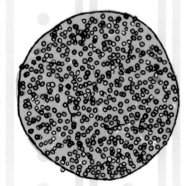

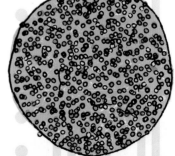

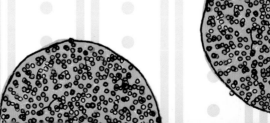

1   1   3

This edition published by Parragon Books Ltd in 2014 and distributed by

Parragon Inc.
440 Park Avenue South, 13th Floor
New York, NY 10016
www.parragon.com/lovefood

LOVE FOOD is an imprint of Parragon Books Ltd

ISBN 978-1-4723-4054-2

Printed in China

New recipes by Angela Drake
Additional photography by Ian Garlick
Illustrations by Charlotte Farmer

Notes for the Reader
This book uses standard kitchen measuring spoons and cups. All spoon and
cup measurements are level unless otherwise indicated. Unless otherwise
stated, milk is assumed to be whole, eggs are large, and individual vegetables
are medium. Unless otherwise stated, all root vegetables should be peeled prior
to using.

Garnishes, decorations, and serving suggestions are all optional and not
necessarily included in the recipe ingredients or method. The times given
are only an approximate guide. Preparation times differ according to the
techniques used by different people and the cooking times may also vary from
those given. Optional ingredients, variations, or serving suggestions have not
been included in the time calculations.